D1430704

Edward Hyams was working on a new biography of Proudhon when he died in late 1975. He lived and worked in Suffolk. He had been an operative in a cigarette factory, written advertising copy, driven a lorry, worked as a gardener, been a business executive, all as a means of financing his writing until he had enough success to live by it. He wrote filmscripts, radio and TV plays, novels, social histories, biographies and books on his favourite art, which he also practised – gardening.

He was the first winner of the Scott Moncrieff Prize for the best translation of the year, Régine Pernoud's *Jeanne d'Arc*.

Edward Hyams

The Changing Face of Britain

PALADIN
GRANADA PUBLISHING
London Toronto Sydney New York

Published by Granada Publishing Limited
in Paladin Books 1977
Reprinted 1979

ISBN 0 586 08258 1

First published in Great Britain by
Kestrel Books 1974 under the title
The Changing Face of England
Copyright © Edward Hyams 1974

Granada Publishing Limited
Frogmore, St Albans, Herts AL2 2NF
and
3 Upper James Street, London W1R 4BP
1221 Avenue of the Americas, New York, NY 10020, USA
117 York Street, Sydney, NSW 2000, Australia
100 Skyway Avenue, Toronto, Ontario, Canada M9W 3A6
110 Northpark Centre, 2193 Johannesburg, South Africa
CML Centre, Queen & Wyndham, Auckland 1, New Zealand

Made and printed in Great Britain by
Richard Clay (The Chaucer Press) Ltd
Bungay, Suffolk
Set in 'Monophoto' Ehrhardt

Contents

For Ann and Feridun Ala with affectionate regard

1 The Raw Material

Britain on the surface is a man-made land: the features of its face as we see it now have been formed by shepherds and farmers, road-, rail- and canal-makers, builders and landscapers and foresters. Even under the skin it has been so quarried and mined and tunnelled, and the spoil of all that burrowing has been so piled and accumulated, that the substance of Britain has been as much worked on as a stone by a sculptor. From the moment when men first began to live on Britain's face, to crawl all over it, dig into it and alter it to suit their comfort and purposes, we have treated its fabric as a craftsman treats his raw material. What was this lump of raw material and what did it look like before the transforming industry of forty or fifty centuries had worked it over, what did it look like before the labour of four or five thousand years began?

One must, however sketchily, begin at the beginning, with the planet Earth a whirling ball of incandescent liquid and gas held together by the inward pull of its own mass and motion, a spherical inferno. On its surfaces – if one can think of surfaces in this context – are deposited, as they rise from the blazing depths, a scum, as fat rises and bubbles to the surface of a pot of boiling stock. This scum congeals – cooling through hundreds of millions of years – so as to hold the great, dense bulk of the planet, mostly molten iron and nickel, in a shell of stone. The shell is in two layers, the inner hollow sphere of basalt – a stone with iron in it and alumino-silicates of sodium and potassium and much besides; the outer hollow sphere becomes the granite foundation stone of the primal land masses.

Those huge, hard, corrugated slabs of granite wrapped round the hollow sphere of basalt, part molten, part solid as the millions of years passed, and within which persisted the unthinkably hot, seething furnace of liquid metal, were subject to colossal forces of wear and tear, were buckled and battered and ground by unimaginably enormous pressures from within; and were planed and filed, flaked and powdered by the heat of the sun throughout the day, by bitter frost of the night, by

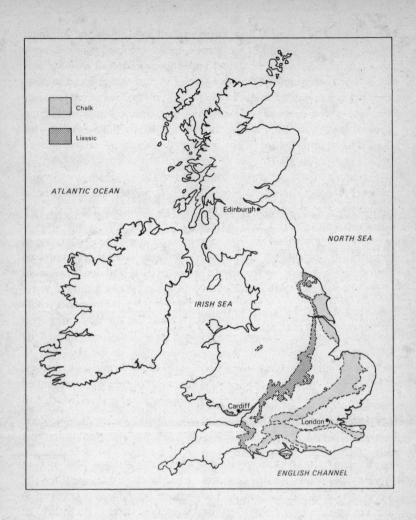

Distribution of Chalk and Lias in England.

ice and water and wind. Those forces worked together on the substance of the Earth: heat expanded the granite, cold contracted it; it was, so to speak, bent and straightened, bent and straightened until its outer surfaces began to crumble. Skin after skin of granite was reduced to powder, which was washed from the heights into the hollows, from land into sea, and settled down as sediment through the waters and there, compressed for millions of years by its own weight, by the weight of what was always being added to it and by the weight of water, formed sedimentary rocks which were to be the stuff of new land masses.

So, much of the foundation stone of Britain was made by physical violence: the swift, catastrophic violence of landslide and avalanche of stone; the fearful uproar of earthquake and eruption; the long, slow violence of erosion. But mere physical forces were not the only ones at work: there was chemistry too. Some of the powdered substance of primal land was soluble. The coarse, insoluble material was compressed into sandstones; or it was accumulated and pressed into dense masses of clay. Those parts which dissolved in water precipitated when the water became over-saturated with them, and formed the soft limestones (chalk included), some of which were later pressed by the giant forces of seismic disturbances into marbles. Often those limestones formed by precipitation contained in their substance the shelly skeletons of countless billions of what were once microscopic living sea-creatures, the *foraminiferae*; or the precipitation formed those igneous rocks called dolerites later to be thrust out through the new stone skins which had covered them, as volcanic lava.

The clay called Lias on the map – you will find one mass of it along the Dorset coast – bluish-grey, crumbling stuff, was deposited by broad, shallow rivers full of the debris of rotting primal hills, rich in fossils, the bodies of sea-creatures, plant and animal, petrified by chemistry and time. For scores of millions of years life was confined to the sea and the land offered nothing to living creatures. Part, then, of one course of the stone and clay that Britain is founded on was made of the countless dead of the first living creatures. There is something oppressive, almost frightening, in this spectacle of the patient accumulation of matter: England, under the skin, is a huge rubbish-heap of crumbled congealed magma and dead bodies, pressed into stone over countless millions of years.

The Britain which was to be our raw material was much longer in the making than it has been in man's time. Its shape might be implicit but was not realized: now it was part of one continent, now of another;

Above: *dolerite, a rock volcanic in origin. It forms the Great Whin Shill along which part of the Roman Wall was built. Below: granite, sedimentary rock formed from coastal or desert sand-dunes. This specimen is known as Bunter sandstone.*

now it was a mountain range, now lost at the bottom of a sea; now a bank accumulating the silt of huge continental rivers, now itself a source of silt material. Thus, for example, the New Red Sandstone of the midlands was once the bottom and beaches of a vast shallow lake under a sun as hot as in the tropics. And there was no green; the land looked like what it was, the product of huge seismic and meteorological catastrophes. If you ever see a lava-field, product of relatively recent volcanic eruption – as you can in the Canary Islands – you will get some small idea of that ancient England's nightmarish desolation. Time and again, the land was made only to be destroyed, buried beneath a falling range of mountains, drowned beneath a sea which, drying out over another few score millions of years, left it with another, different layer of sediment or detritus. Yet each stage in this process of global violence left its traces and is for ever some bit of Britain.

Go back to the inferno under our feet, physical justification, had he known it was there, for the geography and climate of the hell of the old Christian's guilty imagination. There were always places where the skin containing those millions of cubic miles of molten stone was thin. Let it wear too thin, and the boiling, incandescent stuff burst out, buckling and heaving up the solid land, boiling the sea into steam, forcing mountain ranges apart and letting drop the whole provinces which lay between them, belching out into turbulent seas of liquid, seething, glowing and stinking molten stone, to flow in slow tides across the land; and to remain when stilled by cold – ugly and black and dead. We do not think of earthquake and volcano in the British Isles. But they were once an act in the making of the land. All Northern Ireland was a sea of white-hot lava about fifteen million years ago; you can see some of it congealed, still uncovered by the soft skin of vegetation covering most of the land in the Giants' Causeway. Bits of England, Scotland and Wales are made of this lava which boiled out of great crevices and spread and humped over the older courses of stone. Once, long ago, the magma pushed its way up below the surface of Devon and Cornwall, South Wales and parts of Scotland, so buckling and creasing the sedimentary rocks and primal clays of all the west country – a west country still part of a vast land area connected with America – that it crumpled all that land as you might a sheet of paper in your hand. And the crumpling was a new range of mountains. The sort of pressures required to do work on that scale are impossible to imagine except by looking at what they accomplish, not simply in big ways like the heaving up of whole provinces into new shapes, but in detail, at the points of strain – where soft chalks and

The Giants' Causeway in Northern Ireland, formed by the congealing of hot lava about fifteen million years ago. This section shows the strange formations created by the congealing rock.

other limestones were compressed into hard marbles, crumbling sandstones into dense quartzites or other sediments into shales and slates.

When you force a flat sheet of any matter of a certain thickness into corrugations, it will be strained to thinness, and therefore weakness, at the points of bending. In what was to become England's west country, and in other similar parts of Britain too, the molten, unimaginably hot matter under the skin of the earth forced its way through those weak points, spread to form molten plateaux and solidified as the cold worked on it, like a lake freezing into a sheet of ice. Then for tens of millions of years the older, softer surface material all round it was sun-burnt, rain-washed, wind-blown – in short, eroded grain by grain, the hills and mountains planed and sand-blasted down to a level again, gouged out into hollows between the harder stone thrown up by that ancient eruption, that igneous rock which, because it was tougher, endured: all Dartmoor, Bodmin Moor and the Scilly Isles are made of that rock.

It was during such violent upheavals as threw up the igneous rock, and the awful heat of the inner earth working near to the surface, that rock fissures were filled with metallic ores, exploded into them as incandescent liquid, even as gases, by the infernal blast – gases of copper, tin, silver, gold. There they liquefied, solidified, underwent new violences, were turned over, shifted, but were still there for men to find tens of millions of years later.

Is it possible to get any idea of the age of the raw land we were ultimately to use and make into the England we are familiar with? Geologists have made estimates which are perhaps near to the truth but the figures they give us are too enormous to mean anything. The foundation of Wales's hills and green valleys, for example, was laid between three and four hundred million years ago. Perhaps it may be easier to grasp what this implies if we say that the Welsh mountains were then probably higher than the Himalayas are today and that they have been worn down to the pleasing stumps they are now by wind and water; envisage the time it would take to wear Everest down to Snowdon with nothing but snow, rain and wind-blown sand as your tools.

Alternating with the colossal violences in the work of making England were the long stillnesses, intolerably slow unless we mentally hasten them and see the slow fall of chalk specks through the still, warm waters as a sort of blizzard of snow lasting about a hundred million years and forming deep drifts which became countries. And then, there are those pieces of England made of the dead bodies of very small animals: these are the organic limestones. There is, for example, Wenlock Edge

Ammonite, a marine fossil.

in Shropshire which began as a vast coral bed in a warm shallow sea, and is founded on the bodies of myriads of trilobites and other such small marine animals: thus the shales are the product of silting over millions of years which, for example, built up all the land round Ludlow.

Towards the end of the Devonian Age, the age when the old red sandstone was made, living creatures, until then confined to the sea, began to take a hand in land-building, less passive than their predecessors, who had contributed only their dead bodies. As far as we yet know, vegetation, like animal life, begins in the sea with the algae and other seaweeds. The first land plants developed into mosses, ferns and horsetails, the flowerless 'lower plants', many of them as big as trees. As they died and decayed, they added the remainder of their substance to the soil or, slowly transformed by chemistry and pressure, became the coal-layers just as, in those parts of the world where there is oil, its source was the bodies of minute animals. Vegetable carrion, mingling with the small particles of stone which were the products of erosion, became the granular skin of the earth, growing deeper century by century. Washed off the hills and into the valleys, carried by rivers to form alluvial silts, blown by great winds to pile up as loess (although that is one process which did not contribute much to the building of Britain),

A fossil fern from the carboniferous era (coal measure).

the soil accumulated and provided a rich medium for the lives of new kinds of plants. The first land animals to squirm ashore – derived from the lunged fishes – died and, like the plants, contributed the substance of their bodies to make the earth of Britain.

There was no steady, unbroken progress towards the Britain that was to come out of all this. There were setbacks: earthquake and eruption reshaped parts of the land, and slow covering of the newly heaved-up stone formed of vomited magma had to be done over again; the sea covered what was already made land, whole regions were lost under water and, again, what had been forests were made into coal as the land built up above the carrion of gigantic ferns and horsetails. Ages of aridity alternated with ages of humidity. All England, lowland Scotland and the Welsh valleys, barring the mountainous areas and a few other islands, was covered with shallow water which, as it evaporated, laid down the Durham and Cheshire salt-beds. During the Cretaceous Age of some thirty million years, when Britain was still joined to North America (although slowly the Atlantic was driving its waters between the great mass of Greenland and the body of Europe), all but the highest land of Britain lay under salt water; and the chalk downs were deposited grain by tiny grain.

As the land re-emerged from the sea, a new age of vegetation began, with 'higher', flowering plants, the trees more or less as we know them instead of tree-ferns, giant mosses and horsetails. But there were yet more huge disturbances, more earthquakes and volcanoes and overwhelming waters. The giant reptiles had their day, the first big elephantine mammals theirs; and at last the smaller mammals, man's ancestors among them. Long ages of tropical warmth were succeeded by the four glacial periods, separated by the warmer interglacials, which all together make up the Pleistocene Ice Age. Ice covered Britain and its face was gouged, ground, pressed and filed into something like the shape we know, by mighty glaciers which slowly moved southward and as slowly retreated.

From this point we can go more slowly, can start counting in thousands, or at all events in tens of thousands of years. Approximately 20,000 years ago began that 'interglacial' – a warmer period between two glacial ages – which has contained most of the history of mankind as we recognize and understand the word; the prehistory and history, that is, of people much like ourselves, although man had been in being for more than twenty times as long, and perhaps fifty times as long. We say or read almost every day something about the speed of technological and social change – of what we hope is progress: it has not always been so: for perhaps a million and a half years our remote ancestors, Australopithecan and Pithecanthropan man, scarcely changed their ways; Neanderthal man was less conservative, keeping to almost the same ways for about 150,000 years; but men of our own kind have come from hunters armed with sticks to spacemen in under 20,000.

The sea of ice covering most of the northern hemisphere including Britain began to contract, the glaciers to shrink. It was not a steady or continuous process; sometimes the ice lingered at the same terminal line for centuries, or even advanced again a little. But, over all that period of 20,000 years the retreat of the ice continued, jerkily, until it reached roughly the present Polar territory; and the glaciers vanished from Britain, and all Europe, except the Alps and a few Scandinavian mountains.

Clear, then, of ice, but still under its near influence while the Polar ice-cap was more extensive than it is today, Britain was a cold land, all tundra, a sort of island Siberia of bleak, windswept grassland with a sparse population of very hardy trees – pine, birch and willow. About half-way through this period of slow warming up, more broad-leaved

Beech trees, which came later on in the new wave of trees into a warmer Britain.

deciduous trees began to find England a possible place to live in. As melting ice raised the level of the sea, the long hollow of land joining England to the Continent was filled with water and that, at last, made Britain a true island; and therefore warmer.

For water temperature is more stable than land temperature, so that islands are never either quite as cold or quite as hot as great land masses. Oak, then elm, invaded from the south, and in time formed great forests; and somewhere around 1000 B.C., say 3,000 years ago, they were joined by the beech.

The tree species which dominated the face of England, before the broad-leaved species which had solved the problem of winter cold by shedding their leaves and going into dormancy, was the Scotch Pine, *Pinus sylvestris.* The vernacular name is significant. It retreated northward while the deciduous trees moved in from the south and invaded Scotland (while all England and Wales were free of it) until it had become a dominant species in Scotland where the most ancient and lovely specimens of this beautiful but sombre conifer can still be seen in the Great Glen.

It is easy to write in that airy fashion of trees invading, advancing, retreating, as if they could march like the soldiers of an army. The way it works is this: a given species, be it pine, oak, elm or ash, can flourish only in certain soils, between certain extremes of temperature, and given a certain minimum or maximum annual rainfall; this is because those limits define the conditions in which the species evolved. If those particular conditions of soil and climate had never existed, then the species in question would never have come into existence. But living creatures, plants or animals, evolve under the pressures of their environment, to which they are continuously trying to adapt themselves; and those pressures are greatest at the limits of the territory, where the conditions are less nearly those which the species prefers. It is this business of continuous evolution which is associated with the territorial expansion of such species as oak, elm and beech into England.

As the climate grew slowly warmer, seedlings springing from seeds dropped by the trees in the very front line of the advance tended to survive instead of perishing; but because the conditions were, at that limit, still only marginally satisfactory, only the most rugged seedlings survived. Now, that saving ruggedness might, in a few cases, be due to a genetical mutation; that is to say, the seedling might have undergone a small but fundamental change from the nature of its parents, developing the character called hardiness. And that, of course, made it able to flourish in slightly different, less favourable, conditions than those required by its parents and ancestors; moreover, since the change was genetical, the new tree would transmit its hardiness to its own offspring. So, two factors were at work advancing the northern limit of the territory for oak and elm and later beech, in England: climatic change towards mildness; and evolution of the tree species towards hardiness.

Then there is the business of crossing water. It is probably true to say that a majority of the species of plants now growing in England were brought across the water by man. Before man started to interfere in this way, there were only natural causes at work: tree seeds with hard shells can float great distances, even in sea water, and remain viable; the seeds in many tree fruits eaten by birds pass through the birds undamaged. The processes of natural generation of forests are slow, certainly; but by comparison with the pace of geological events glanced at above, they are like lightning.

While the new species were moving into England and Wales from the south, the old tundra species, under precisely the same kinds of influence, were retreating northward into Scotland: at their southern limit conditions were too mild to suit them or they were crowded out by the newly advancing species; at their northern limit conditions were becoming more favourable and they could begin to advance towards the Pole. Birch might survive in England on soils too light to suit oaks, and perhaps willow in soils too wet; but the pine, for example, surviving in harsher Scotland, became extinct in England which was left without evergreen conifers.

2   Hunters and Farmers

Mankind's prehistory is the period before the invention of writing; his history is the period from the invention of writing until now. His prehistory is approximately twenty times as long as his history and during most of it, before he learned to farm, he got his living like the other mammals, by gathering and eating the roots, seeds and leaves of plants and by hunting other animals, birds and fishes for meat. Living thus like an animal, although feeling and thinking increasingly like a man, he made no more lasting impression on the face of the land than the wolves or tigers; and rather less than some of the other animals, for large herds of deer and wild cattle can alter the vegetation of a whole region.

The first men to reach Britain, at a time when it was not separated from the continental mainland by water, belonged to the species called Pithecanthropus; the only evidence of their presence here is a piece of a skull which was found when a gravel-pit was being dug at Swanscombe in the Thames Valley. There may, at their zenith in an England otherwise quite empty of men about a quarter of a million years ago, have been about two hundred of these Pithecanthropi. If they made any mark at all on the land's face, it was no more than a pit or two, laboriously dug with pointed sticks, big shells and bare hands, to trap animals for food.

After Pithecanthropus came Neanderthal man (named after the Neanderthal valley in Germany where the first skeleton of this race of men was found). Neanderthal men came into England, following herds of game-animals, not much less than 150,000 years ago, during the last ('Wurmian') Ice Age, into a cold, bleak land most of which was covered with glacier ice hundreds of feet thick. But they had fire round which they could huddle in caves against the bitter cold. These men were hunters; and they were tool- and weapon-makers using wood and flint for their materials. Yet, although certainly more numerous than their predecessors, they were no more capable of making an impression on the face of Britain and they left it as unchanged as Africa by the great apes.

Plaster head of Neanderthal Man as he might have looked.

Few moments in the history of the human race – and although he was not of our species, Neanderthal man was a member of the human race – appear to me more poignant than that of the encounter between the wandering groups of dim-minded, shambling Neanderthalers and the new kind of men who came into England from the south-east. The Neanderthaler stood, indeed, on his feet and used his hands like a man; but he was graceless. Like all very ugly creatures – like Caliban in *The Tempest*, who is surely a great poet's 'recollection' of him – he seems pitiful and, to us, pathetic. Did he have a language? Some kind of speech, probably, but very simple and very limited: and since it is on the complexity and subtlety of language that we depend for abstract thought, and therefore for any apprehension of the world which goes beyond the immediate sense reactions, a people without a fully developed language would be scarcely human as we understand the word.

How did the new kind of men who now began to visit, if not settle, in England (for the Channel was not yet filled with water; and even when it was, that water was much narrower than it is now; and in any case the new men soon had boats), how did this new race come into existence? Almost certainly as a mutation occurring either in a group of Neanderthalers, or in a group of some ancestor common to Neanderthalers and the new men – Pithecanthropus, perhaps. However and wherever these people came into being, they were our own direct ancestors, and so in all respects like ourselves. No longer ape-like, they had fully human faces, with no more body hair than we have; they carried themselves erect and moved not in a shamble but lightly and easily. They have been given a name, Cro-Magnon, after the place in France where the first skulls of their kind were found.

And this race of men still survives. For when, early in the fifteenth century, the Norman adventurer Jean de Bethencourt started the conquest of the Canary Islands, the natives which he and the Spaniards who came after him had to overcome were a race of white-skinned, often fair-haired and blue-eyed savages, in a late prehistoric cultural stage. And in the nineteenth century it was discovered that their skulls were identical with those of Cro-Magnon man and had a peculiarity in the shape of certain teeth shared only with Cro-Magnon man.[1] And since these people were not completely exterminated by the Spaniards, and often intermarried with them, there is Cro-Magnon blood in the present-day Canary Islanders.

What did the poor Neanderthalers think of these new men when they first set eyes on them? Did they recognize kinship with such radiant beings? And what, for their part, did the new people make of those lumbering, beast-like half-men? We can learn nothing about the nature and feelings of this encounter from what we know of first meetings between civilized people and primitive savages in historical times, such as the encounter between Europeans and Australian aborigines. The most primitive savages surviving into historical times were of the same species as ourselves, differing only in being less advanced technologically; there is an infallible test: all the surviving 'races' of mankind are inter-fertile. Apparent, but merely apparent, differences have been created by the fact that in civilized communities every generation of men since the beginning of our race has been born richer in accumulated knowledge and skills than its predecessor. I can best express this identity in this way: if you had taken a child from among the most primitive savages ever discovered by explorers, *or a child of the Cro-Magnon people who began to come into Britain about 12,000 years ago*, at birth, brought it up like a child of your own in your own family, and sent it to school with your own children, that child would have been capable of learning as much and as quickly as your own children. But a Neanderthal child would not, any more than a baby orang-utan can, after the third year, keep up with the human baby whom it has been reared with since birth, though the Neanderthal baby would have got much further in the curriculum than the baby ape.

[1] In all the races of men we know excepting these Canary Islanders the canine teeth are longer than the rest. The Cro-Magnon people had canines level with the other teeth; so do many Canary Islanders even now; the skulls of the Guanches, aboriginal Canary Islanders, all show this peculiarity.

These new men, last splendid flower of the Old Stone Age were, like their predecessors, hunters but, being more numerous and cleverer, were capable of making an impression on their environment in at least one way – by over-hunting some particular species of animal for the food and raw material – hide, horn and bone – yielded by its body. Nowadays we are very conscious of the damage we do in exterminating beautiful species of animals and hold international conferences about it: but man's impact on his fellow animals is no new thing; it began to do damage at least twenty thousand years ago, although it did not reach catastrophic proportions until about A.D. 1600. How could Stone Age men do real damage with such relatively poor weapons and other means as they had? By rounding up and then slaughtering large herds of game, far beyond their immediate needs. We know from historical examples what savages no better armed than they were can do: in New Zealand between c. A.D. 900, when they colonized the islands, and the eighteenth century, when Captain Cook arrived, the Polynesians had made extinct at least twenty species of large birds, which they had found there when they came. It is possible that Cro-Magnon man wiped out the European rhinoceros.

But nothing like that happened in Britain, not at first, if only because the hunting parties which came over from France were few and small, there was nothing to attract them except the huge herds of game and they might, like Tacitus thousands of years and hundreds of Continental invasions later, have said that the climate, though it did not suffer from extremes of heat or cold, was unpleasant.

At the end of the last chapter we had the tundra flora receding northward and hardwood forests invading England. We had run ahead of ourselves in time, and must now go backwards and start again, in order to look at what the newcomers saw when they reached Britain. It was a dismal place, still partly covered with glaciers.

When one talks of the 'end' of an Ice Age, that does not mean that suddenly one summer the ice disappeared; it means that the ice had ceased to advance and was beginning to retreat. As it did so it left a mess of scree, bog, mere and fast-running streams, where grass grew, and then the trees we have named, birch, willow and above all pine. It was, however, open country, a sort of badly drained parkland with very few trees, a fact which explains the vast herds of game. It is possible that what first sent hunting parties across to Britain was the advance of the trees farther south in Europe, trees which drove the game herds north-

Neolithic tools,
flint arrowhead and axe.

ward. That advance began with the pines, until all Britain looked like parts of Canada do today. And this meant that the people had to change their ways, for the great herds they had lived on vanished still farther northward; England's happy hunting grounds were no more, while they still survived in Scotland and perhaps, the Welsh highlands.

So the next wave of migrants into Britain found open country only along the coasts, along river banks, and on the chalk downs and other places where the soil was too thin for trees to get a footing. There was no respite from the slow and overwhelming march of the trees, for as the improving climate – we have seen this in Chapter 1 – forced the pines to the north, so it let in the deciduous hardwoods from the south.

Men could still, of course, be hunters in the woods, but the game was small and more difficult to drive and even to find. Once again the people lived by gathering shellfish and birds' eggs, roots and berries, seeds and mushrooms. But although stone tools became much smaller, on the whole equipment was better, more diverse, more thoughtfully designed. And fishing became so important that fishing-gear improved. We are now in what is called Mesolithic Britain, no longer the Old Stone Age;

there had been a sort of industrial revolution; or rather evolution, since it had been long and gradual. The people must have got a fair living, for they were able to spread up from the south all along the east coast into Scotland, and up the west coast into Wales as well. Nearly all movement was along the shores or river valleys, for not only was woodland undergrowth an obstacle when your tools were of stone, but the forest was sombre and forbidding.

And now at last men began very slightly to change the look of Britain's face. Although most of the tools made by Mesolithic man were small (microliths), they did have a big stone axe capable of felling trees, though it must have been a laborious business. Or, rather, some of the tribes did. So small clearings appeared among the trees especially in the south and south-east; there were more boats on rivers and lakes and coastal waters; a few simple huts were built.

It is important to recall how slowly the changes we have been describing took place. For example, we can safely say that they would not have been noticed within one person's lifetime; perhaps, if anyone lived into old age in those days, there were old people who vaguely remembered that once there had been fewer trees and more water in the landscape, and who shook their heads over the dwindling of the game herds as over an irreparable disaster; perhaps, many generations later, there were other old people who recalled that in *their* childhood there had been more pine trees and fewer oak trees. Until very recently, to each generation the Britain they inherited seemed immemorial and eternal. It never was, of course; but life is short and natural changes very long indeed. And until the coming of the next wave of invaders, it was always the land's slow change that forced change on the people, never the people who forced change on the land.

To understand what happened next we have to turn our attention far away from Britain. I do not want here to examine the reasons why it was in certain parts of the Middle East that people were first encouraged to pass from the clever-animal role of hunter–gatherer, in order to get a living, to the human role of food producer. It will be sufficient to say that the people of those Middle Eastern regions were not cleverer than anybody else; and that certain particularly favourable conditions led to the first successful farming and domestication of useful animals which had, till then, merely been hunted. There must have been people in very many parts of the world who noticed and, after thought, understood the implications of the sprouting of seeds which had been gathered for food and had become damp in storage. It is one thing to realize that it would be better to plant and reap food grains at home, than go wandering all over the place looking for them. It is quite another, given the conditions in which people lived in Britain 7–8,000 years ago, to do anything about it. At all events, while here and in most of the rest of the world men were continuing their immemorial hunting ways, the Middle East people learned (and the lesson was learned surprisingly quickly) how to grow plant foods, and how to herd sheep and goats, later cows and horses, instead of hunting them.

The invention of farming and stock-breeding spread in two ways: by imitation and by immigration. People living next door to the lands of the first farmers would have tried the new ways for themselves, and as the farmers grew stronger on the new wealth which farming enabled them to accumulate, some of their neighbours may even have had farming forced on them, much as 'emergent' nations are having industrialization forced on them now. But it was very far from being as simple as that: in the two great centres where farming was so successful that their communities became very rich, villages developed into great cities and civilization began, very special conditions made that advance possible. These two places were the land between the rivers Tigris and Euphrates, and the Nile valley; and in both of them the soil was renewed annually by silt-laden floods, so that continuous cultivation could not exhaust it. In most other places farmers could not settle down on one site and till it year after year: before the invention of manuring, soils deteriorated within a few seasons; the first farmers could only scratch its surface with their poor hand tools. Consequently the first farmers away from those two great alluvial centres had to keep on the move, seeking new land. The movement outwards from the centre of invention was like the slow tides of an infinite series of small waves.

It was, then, something like 5,000 years after the beginnings of farming in the Middle East that the first waves of the tide of farming peoples washed up on the shores of England. About 2500 B.C., boats carrying cattle as well as men, sheep, goats, later the bigger cattle and pigs, and, of course, domestic dogs and a few bags of seed-corn, found moorings on the south-east coast. Their people, always turning their backs on the dark forests which covered so much of the land, sought the thin, treeless chalk downs, the limestone ridges and plateaux. Sussex and all Wessex were their first home, and as they prospered moderately, they pushed up into Norfolk and Lincolnshire, and even into Yorkshire and the lowlands of Scotland.

Windmill Hill, showing the famous bell barrows.

Their small scratchings of arable, their scattering of huts and boats, were not the most impressive marks these people made on the land. On the tops of many hills they built big concentric earthwork enclosures, which were also fenced with wood, as corrals for their cattle. There, every late autumn, the greater part of their animals had to be slaughtered, for they had no means to feed a large number over the winter; in fact, no means of over-wintering large numbers of cattle were found for another 3,000 years, or thereabouts.

These great cattle-corrals were not the only permanent 'buildings' left by the Windmill Hill people, for they also built the imposing graves called Long Barrows, long, narrow walled passages built up of turves and stones and covered with more turves, some of them over 100 yards long, many a third of that size. They were communal graves: when one

The Earth Mother: the great goddess worshipped by the first farmers and even the first industrial workers. In primitive representations her maternal attributes are grossly exaggerated but her form slowly evolved under the hands of artists into such glorious works of art as the Venus of Milo.

of the people died, the grave was opened and he or she was carried in to join their dead fellow-tribesmen. But perhaps those structures were not only graves, but something like temples, places of worship, or, at least, holy places. All those early farmers who had moved up Europe's river valleys and down them to the sea, and into England, were worshippers of Earth, in the form of a woman, the Earth Mother, the Great Goddess, who in time acquired many names – Tanit, Isis, Astarte, Aphrodite, Venus and yet more. Perhaps the long earth passage – in Britain a poor copy of the Continental megalithic graves built of stone – was an image of the womb: from the mother you came; to the mother you returned; there was no death, only a cycle of eternal life.

What means to do their work did these people have? Earthenware for their stores and their cooking had already been invented. Flint and other kinds of stone were still the materials of their cutting tools, and in getting them they set another kind of mark on Britain's face. Whereas their predecessors had been content to pick up flint on the surface, these

The ancient craft of flint mining at Brandon, Essex, which still goes on. This is the interior of a workshed photographed in 1922 with the flint workers doing their job by ancient methods.

people dug for it and were our first miners. Their mining tool was a deer antler used, no doubt, as a pick. They dug pits in the Sussex and Wiltshire downs.

But not all the mining done here was of this open-cast type, even then. In East Anglia there were people, either natives or immigrants from north Europe, who were not farmers but Mesolithic hunters to begin with, but who became the first industrial specialists in this country. Their flint mining and manufacturing industry, made prosperous by the demand from the few farmers for heavy axes to deal with the trees, was centred on the place called Grimes Graves, in Suffolk. These deep pits were not graves, they were flint mines; and for that matter still are, for this most ancient industry is still at work there. The big nodules of easily worked flint were brought to the surface and made into axes which were traded all over southern England; it is even possible that there was a small export trade to France and the Low Countries.

This was one of the first two instances of men in Britain getting their food not by hunting, gathering or producing it by farming or raising stock, but by buying it from the producers in exchange for the product of their industry. Until then each man made his own tools and weapons, although doubtless some were better at the work than others and might be persuaded to make them for their friends as well.

That these old miners thought of their craft exactly as if they were producing food directly is clear. For, deep in one of the flint pits, was found a figure of the Earth Mother goddess: she was:

> ... enthroned above a pile of antlers on which rested a chalk-carved phallus. The shrine had been set up in one of the few pits which by chance had failed to strike the flint bed, and Our Lady of the Flint Mines, it seems, was being asked to cure such sterility.[2]

The next group of immigrants to reach England and spread through Britain were people of a very different temper. They arrived round about 2000 B.C., nearly four thousand years ago, and they were representatives of the Aryan or Indo-European people who started from somewhere in Asia and over-ran all Europe and India (hence Indo-European as the name of the group of languages derived from their original speech). They had bronze as well as stone tools and weapons; they were pastoralists, that is cattle-men. Rich in gear on the produce of their herds, restlessly seeking new lands to expand in, they were warlike, descending like beasts of prey on the pacific farmers to the south and west of their homeland, and spreading, as it must have seemed to these farmers, like a plague for thousands of miles. They were tough, sturdy, clever and they worshipped the sky, as did so many peoples of the great Eurasian steppe. Now whereas, to the best of our knowledge, pre-Aryan Neolithic 'society' was matriarchal, reflecting the worship of the Great Goddess by giving predominance to female values, this new warrior people was patriarchal, reflecting the worship of the sky god who, in time, was to be given almost as many names as his female rival – Brama, Zeus and Jove were three of them.

So, perhaps for the first time, there was colonization-by-warfare in Britain, whose older inhabitants were quite unable to stand up to the fierce energy and superior weapons of the newcomers who seized and held their upland pastures, and who penetrated inland to be absorbed or partially absorbed by the older people with their gentler, subtler ways.

The first wave of Aryans, the pre-Celtic ones, did not, except in one

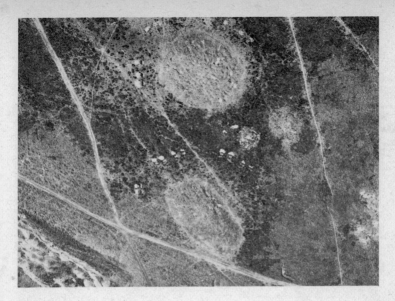

The round barrows of Ditchingham in Norfolk; an aerial view.

important respect, make much more change in the look of Britain than their predecessors had done. They might be better equipped but were not very numerous. Their coming meant that a new kind of mining-scar was made on the land's face, for being bronze-workers they needed copper from the rocks of North Wales, and tin from those of Cornwall, so that two new industries were promoted. These people made no Long Barrows, for they did not practise the communal burial which was part of the Earth Mother cult; instead they made Round Barrows, in which men were buried individually.

They still, on the whole, kept to the treeless grasslands where their cattle could be moved from pasture to pasture. They, too, felled and burned off trees to make themselves more room. But most of the country remained as virgin and empty as present-day Amazonia which also has its small, scattered tribes of primitive hunters. Britain was still a land of interminable dark forests where the voice of man was heard little.

But the new people set one extraordinary mark on the land: their temples of a religion focused on the sky god and the sun. These were the first wrought stone buildings in our country.

The layout of the largest of these temples can still be clearly traced at Avebury; but only in Stonehenge do the ruins of what was, probably,

Above: *the standing stones of Stonehenge, possibly one of the most highly developed astronomical observatories the world has ever known.* Below: *reconstruction of Avebury with its circles of standing stones in place. 'Discovered' in the seventeenth century by John Aubrey, it is now almost completely obliterated, and the village of Avebury itself stands in the middle of the gigantic ring.*

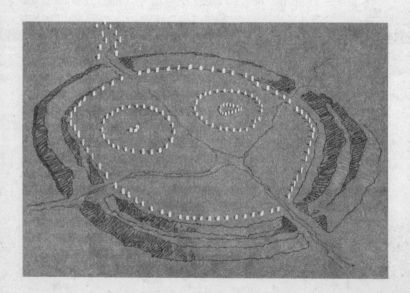

the most important one survive. These two were not, of course, the only ones of their kind; there were smaller ones all over certain parts of Britain even as far north as the Orkneys. But Stonehenge, at the heart of what must have been the most populous part of England at that time, must have been their Canterbury Cathedral. We still know all too little about its significance. For instance, the huge dressed sandstone blocks, with the beautifully cut tenons to steady the massive lintel stones, are of a kind of stone which came from Avebury, only twenty miles away, but the bluish stones of the outer ring (probably the inner ring at the first building, *c*. 1900 B.C., becoming the oter ring at rebuilding *c*. 1500 B.C.) had to be fetched, presumably on rafts by sea, from Pembrokeshire, 200 miles away, the nearest point at which this kind of stone can be found.

Still, then, no great change: a nibbling at the forest edges and a few more clearings; doubtless a reduction in the population of wolves and bears as the new weapons made it easier to deal with them, although it took centuries for metal to oust stone, and there are examples in several parts of Europe of new flint-flaking industries being started up literally hundreds of years after bronze weapons had been in current use and even after iron was beginning to be fairly common. A few more huts were built, a few more boats crept round the coasts and explored the islands; the herds of cattle increased; and there were the great temples, usually of wood, probably, or undressed stone, but on the same model as Stonehenge. From the air the Britain of 1500 B.C. must, but for a scar here and there, a few drifts of smoke from burning woods, and the long shadow of a sarsen stone, have still looked very like the Britain of 3000 B.C., an empty land of great forests, vast marshes, and broad, grassy hills.

The Celts began to reach England from France and Belgium some centuries before the first Roman reconnaissance-in-strength led by Julius Caesar. It is a curious fact that we have for centuries persisted in the mistake of identifying the short, dark people in our population, especially in Wales and the highlands of Scotland, as the Celtic strain. It is nothing of the sort; those people have an older ancestry, their colouring and stature is a heritage from the early Mediterranean farmers who came here long before anyone had ever heard of the Celts.

The incomers did to the men in possession what was, much later, to be done to them: drove most of them west and north into the difficult hill country, so as to have the easier lowlands for themselves. I do not know if the Celts had any distinguishing physical characteristics, but if

Fyfield Down in Wiltshire, an aerial view of rectangular Celtic fields, showing the striations caused by many centuries of furrows ploughed over this ancient land.

they did they were those of tall stature, physical strength and either fair or reddish hair. Whatever they looked like, these Continental invaders made more impression on the land's face than all the peoples who had come before them into Britain.

The semi-nomadic farmer–stock-breeders of all the previous immigrants had scratched their miserable patches of arable by hand. The Celts brought with them an invention ancient in the east, but new to Britain: the ox-drawn plough. Now this tool is not absolutely necessary to the development of a rich economy or the growth of civilization: the Andean farmers had no plough until the arrival of the Spaniards in the sixteenth century, yet they built a high civilization, great cities, roads and canals, and accumulated the enormous wealth of the Inca empire on a foundation of hand tools. But to do that calls for a kind of social organization which is very difficult to bring about among fiercely individual worshippers of sky gods and the male principle. So the coming of the plough to Britain made an enormous difference. Yet I do not think that it can have been the plough which enabled the new immigrants to settle in one place, till the same fields year after year, and therefore build not temporary shelters but permanent villages; and remember that the village is the beginning of civilization. Athens and Rome were villages once, like Canterbury and London which these Celts founded in England. These new Englishmen must have brought with them something even more important than the plough: the knowledge that by manuring a field you can go on using it for ever and need not move every few seasons to a new site. Without this knowledge no such social stability as came to Britain with the Celts would have been possible, especially on the light soils which were the only ones the Celtic plough enabled them to exploit.

At this point England was half in the Stone Age, half in the Bronze Age, and on the verge of the Iron Age.

This was soon true also of the Welsh valleys and Scottish lowlands, as of parts of Ireland; but this first industrial revolution was slower to spread into the highlands. Topography was not the only difficulty: there was already a cultural barrier. For the first time permanent farms were made and passed from father to son. The first Celtic immigrant settlers were probably using bronze; but by about 500 B.C. came people who nderstood the smelting and working of iron. And as that doubtless very expensive metal became more and more important, there was a change in the industrial scarring of Britain's face. Iron ore was not found in the same places as copper or tin, but much farther east. The workings of flint in East Anglia, igneous rock in the north-west, copper in Wales and tin in Cornwall, were not suddenly abandoned, of course. There are analogues to what happened in our own time, provided we remember that things move a thousand times faster now: for example, the running down of the coal-mining industry because of the rise in importance of oil and natural gas as energy-producing fuels. So there was a gradual decline in the working of flint and the mining of tin and copper, a gradual rise in the working of the iron ore in the forest of Dean and later in the Sussex–Kent weald. There was no run-down in the Welsh goldfields, of course. There is a lot to reflect on in the fact that the one metal-extraction industry which has never suffered a decline as a consequence of technological advance is the one concerned with the production of the only metal which is, if not actually useless, at least very dispensable: gold.

Above: *the beautiful, formal white horse of Westbury in Wiltshire carved in the chalk hillside. It can be seen for miles around. The figures of two children walking along its underside can barely be seen against its gigantic shape.* Below: *the concentric earthworks of Maiden Castle, a Celtic ruin.*

Like their fellow-Aryan predecessors, the Celts were warriors. So, as well as villages which they were the first to build, they built forts. The Windmill Hill people's hill-top earthworks had been cattle corrals. The Celtic earthworks of Maiden Castle, the Wrekin, Chanctonbury and a hundred lesser modifications of England's shape, were military works.

The plough, and the spade of the military pioneer, were at last beginning to enable men to make changes in the look of Britain which really could be seen.

3 The Romans: Roads, Towns and Villas

The last wave of migrant Celts to make their way into England before the Roman Conquest were the Belgae. The land they entered was one of scattered farms and even sparser settled villages in a land that was otherwise almost wholly wild. To get an idea of just how wild and empty of man the country still was, consider that, whereas today's population is about fifty million people, it was then not more than 250,000: for every 200 people now, there was then only one.

In the short time before being overwhelmed by the Romans, the Belgae – Celts from the Low Countries – made a difference. They brought with them a heavy, wheeled plough which could turn over heavy clay loams which were too much for the lighter, older ploughs. They made their farms all over the south-east and as far as the midlands; they built more villages and by the time Claudius landed here with his army in A.D. 43, there were probably more people, 350,000 perhaps. But they were a tiny scattering in a vast wilderness, huddling in their insignificant settlements hacked out of the wild.

For some reason we think of the Roman conquest of Britain – that is, England and Wales – as having been accomplished by Julius Caesar. This is because he was one of those generals who write books about their accomplishments. In fact, his raid on Britain was not really much more than a reconnaissance-in-strength. He defeated some of the Celtic Belgic tribes which, being no more than artistically gifted savages with an archaic technology, were still fighting in chariots like the people of the Middle East some thousand years before; he took notes of the look of the country and its people; but withdrew after imposing a tribute (was it ever paid?) and took no more interest in the place for the rest of his life. After all, he had only recently subdued Gaul and his raid on Britain was not much more than a move in his political game.

The man who really did add Britannia to the Roman Empire was the emperor Claudius, a much abler and cleverer man and a much better soldier than the historians have given him credit for being. The only

Bronze head of the Emperor Claudius, found in the river Alde, Saxmundham, Suffolk; probably from Colchester.

Above: *model of an Iron Age chariot.*

Below: *gold stater minted at Camulodunum (Colchester) during the reign of Cunobelinus (Cymbeline).*

natives who mattered from a military point of view were the Belgic tribes, relatively numerous, living on their herds of cattle and some farming, fine workers in metal and stone, but for the most part savages. Their aristocracy, with connections in Gaul, were to some small extent Latinized: for example, they imported wine, a sure sign of a civilized class. They had no cities, but some of their larger wooden villages might be called 'towns' at a pinch.

Since London is a Celtic name, there must have been one such town in the region of Westminster; but if so it was an inconsiderable place, or so say the archaeologists and prehistorians, a place grown up perhaps because the site was the lowest crossing-place in the course of the

Thames. In other respects it was not at all the sort of site to be chosen as a settlement by the Celtic people or any other kinds of first-century 'English': it was too marshy and, away from the riverside, too heavily wooded.

On the other hand, the Thames was and long had been an easy way into the interior of England, whether for raiders, traders or settlers. Under Roman government the village of London began to grow, however, chiefly as a trading town for merchants from the Continent. But it did not become politically the most important town in England until Queen Boudicca and her charioteers destroyed it during the same campaign in which they destroyed the older Roman capital, Colchester. That being the order of events, we had best glance first at Colchester, and only then at London.

At the very beginning of the first century of our era King Cymbeline (that is, the Belgic prince Cunobelinus), having united all the tribes and territories of the south-east into a kingdom, decided to build himself a capital town on a site near to and south-west of present-day Colchester. A dike and bank for military defence were dug to enclose it and a village settlement of huts built inside it. Although some of the Belgic princes were to some extent Latinized in their ways, they do not seem to have adopted substantial Roman ways of building; their villages were sprawling and probably squalid, though the hall-houses of their chiefs may have had some Roman refinements.

After the emperor Claudius had defeated Cymbeline's son and successor Caractacus, he had this 'town' destroyed, used the site as a brick-field and building-contractor's yard and started building a Roman town nearby. It was chiefly a *colonia* – a settlement for retired soldiers who had been rewarded with money and a grant of land; but the place became their administrative and religious capital, with a grand classical temple to the god Claudius (the deified emperor), built on vaults later used to support the Norman castle which is now the museum. This was the Colchester which Boudicca destroyed after she had massacred the citizens and the garrison. It was rebuilt after her defeat. As London had to be rebuilt at the same time, for the same reason, the job was done so as to make it suitable to be the capital in Colchester's place, presumably for some geographical reason, the Thames being England's most important waterway.

We know how small the city was because its walls, built much later but on the course of the original earthwork, of Kentish ragstone with bonding courses of brick, can still be traced: they enclosed about 330

The Colchester vase.

acres, with gates at Newgate, Aldersgate, Cripplegate, Bishopsgate and Aldgate. The river was bridged to carry the south road into the city, rather to the east of the newest bridge. That was the first London town and, although larger, it was probably very like the other towns which the Romans built in Britain.

Canterbury was another, and more considerable, Belgic village, re-built as a Roman town. When, in the later centuries of the Roman occupation, German sea-rovers began to land, loot and burn in east Kent and all up the east coast, this Saxon shore became a special defence area provided with forts and a fleet, under the unified command of an admiral. Four of these forts defended Canterbury and London: Reculver, near Herne Bay; Richborough, between Sandwich and Ramsgate; Strutfall Castle, near Lympne; and Dover, which was yet another Roman town and, as the nearest harbour to the Gallic ports, a very important one. The Roman lighthouse to guide cross-channel war-ships and merchant shipping is still there, or at all events forty feet of it, octagonal in section, inside Dover Castle. There was no Roman town at Folkestone (that was a later foundation) but two of the hundreds of villas built in Britain during the occupation were there, and their vestiges can be seen on the cliffs above East Wear Bay.

Only Dover, of these four sea-forts, still stands on the sea; the sea has eroded the land all round Reculver; Strutfall has been stranded by the silting up of Lympne Haven; and the sea has withdrawn from

A clay lamp with impressed patterns, found at Verulamium.

Richborough. While men were at last beginning to make some impression on the face of England, nature had not yet finished the job of shaping the land.

One of the most important towns built by the Romans in Britain was Verulamium, near to the present St Albans. The site was chosen by the emperor Claudius because it was already an important Belgic village, capital of one of the princes of the Catevellauni. This Roman city became a self-governing municipium, on the Italian model, the only one in Roman Britain. The first foundation was another of the towns sacked by Boudicca in her great rising, the most ferocious and nearly successful attempt to throw the Romans out of England; but it was rebuilt immediately, increased in wealth and importance, and in A.D. 150 was enriched with a splendid theatre.

The most lasting mark the Romans made on the face of England was, of course, the network of roads, if only because so many modern main roads are built on top of them. Were there roads in England before Rome built them? Tracks, no doubt, but roads, no. It is almost impossible to visualize a roadless England now; but tracks were good enough where the few travelling traders, and such craftsmen as bronzesmiths and blacksmiths, had only to serve a total population of 300–400,000 people. For the Romans it was different; they had disciplined regiments to move as quickly as possible, and communications to maintain between their garrisons.

Above: *the Romans left many more personal mementoes of their stay in Britain. Here is a tombstone of a Roman cavalryman called Rufus Sita.* Below: *the remains of the old Roman road at Blackstone Edge.*

From Dover the well-founded and paved road ran through Canterbury and Rochester, and other Roman towns, to London: the pre-motorway A road runs on top of it, for Roman road-surveying has never been bettered. From London the road ran south-west to Silchester, again an important Roman town, and about five miles west of London a branch turned north to Verulamium. The next considerable town on the southerly branch of the road to the south-west which passed through Old Sarum and Pentridge, and east of modern Blandford, was Dorchester, which the Romans called Dornavaria. It was not the most westerly of their towns: a road from Dorchester went west to rejoin the main road south-east of Hanbury where it had arrived by way of Winterbourne, Wincanton and Chard, which did not then exist of course, and continued west to its teminal at Exeter, or Isca Dumnoniorum, the most westerly example of urbanization in England at this time.

The network of Roman roads outwards from London was complex: you can best study it on the map. The road to Colchester ran through modern Chelmsford and north as far as a terminal, possibly a camp, at Norwich. North it went to Aldborough in the north-east, Isurium Brigantum, which was in the military zone; military, because the constant threat of the Scottish barbarians made it impossible to allow this part of England to relax into the peaceful routine of an ordinary province under civil administration. Then there was York, at first simply a legionary fort, then a city where, in due course, Constantine's legions were to make him emperor, and so enable him to reunite the shattered empire and shift its capital to Byzantium, refounded as Constantinople and to Christianize the Roman world officially.

The reason why the Romans did not carry their conquest into Scotland was not because it was not worth their trouble – the lowlands would have been at least as valuable as Yorkshire and the tribesmen made as good soldiers as the men of other outlying regions of the Empire: no; the Empire was, from the military point of view, over-extended.

Between 79 and 85 A.D., the very able military governor, Agricola, father-in-law of the historian Tacitus, fought his way to and beyond the Highland line, defeated the combined forces of the Pictish and Scottish tribes, while his fleet landed marines to subdue the people who, in Caithness and Orkney, built those 'brochs' – tall stone tower-castles enclosing a courtyard – which were among the earliest man-made marks on Britain's face. But Agricola was one of those commanders whose skill and strength of will give a false impression of his country's strength; when he was recalled, Rome found that she could not afford to hold what he had conquered.

In Wales there was Venta Silurum – now only the village of Caerwent remains – built on a fifty-acre site enclosed by earthworks, and on the grid system, with a forum, baths, a temple, a basilica and a street of shops. The stone walls still partly visible were not added until the third century. Then there was Caerleon, Isca, built as a military camp or fortress, then as a town, headquarters of the 2nd Legion. The soldiers became a part of the life of the town and countryside, many of them married local girls, and married quarters were built for them outside the walls. As well as the usual public buildings, Isca had an amphitheatre for 'games'. Quite a lot of this Roman town survived into the twelfth century and Gerald the Welshman gives an account of it as he saw it 800 years ago:

The city was handsomely built of masonry, with courses of bricks. Many vestiges of its former splendour may yet be seen, in immense palaces with gilded roofs, in imitation of Roman magnificence . . . a town of prodigious size, remarkable hot baths, relics of temples and theatres all enclosed with fine walls. . . . You will find on all sides . . . subterranean buildings, aqueducts, underground passages; and what I think worthy of notice, stoves contrived with wonderful art to transmit the heat insensibly through narrow tubes passing up the side of the walls.

Chester was another such garrison town which became a city and Silchester has already been mentioned. Bath, Aquae Sulis, was a city of a different kind, built because of the hot medicinal springs round its hot bath. Roman Britons went there to take the waters, bathe, rest and play; and no doubt to give expression in their clothes to the latest fashions from Italy. Then, as later, it was a town of physicians and their patients, and of pleasure-seekers. The walled town covered only twenty-three acres but there must have been suburbs for the place to have become as important as it was. It was linked by road to Silchester and to the Exeter road; and to Cirencester – Corinium – with its military barracks, its amphitheatre, its forum and temple. The Roman towns were built to a pattern and were all very much alike: unlike the towns which were to become typical of the British scene, they did not just grow, they were planned, and there was only one plan.

Under the emperor Hadrian, the Romans built a wall to stop the barbar-

Above: *a map of main Roman Roads in Britain.* Below: *the sepulchral slab in memory of another Roman soldier, Caius Valerius Victor, standard-bearer of the Second Legion, found at Caerleon in 1717.*

ian Picts from raiding, looting and burning the Roman province. It extended from the coast west of Carlisle to present-day Newcastle. Behind it was a complex of military camps and small towns, among which Corbridge – Corstopitum – was the administrative and supply centre; others were Ebchester, Binchester and Lanchester. But the wall itself, built between A.D. 122 and 138, first of earthwork, later of stone, with a strong-point and look-out tower every mile of its length, was itself a sort of long, thin town.

It has an exciting history. The completion of the stone building took over a decade; it was all done by 138. In one of his stories recalling England's past, Rudyard Kipling suggested that this last outpost of the empire in the west, the ultimate frontier, was used as a punishment posting: officers who had to be disciplined for some offence or who had, perhaps, made a political blunder by backing the wrong general in the Roman struggle for power, were posted there to serve a term of penance. They were, consequently, a wild lot, drinking heavily, gaming and brawling. It is, of course, only guesswork, but plausible enough. And wild or not, the garrison was effective; not until it was greatly weakened by withdrawals of troops to help one general oust another as emperor on the Continent, did the Scots break through. That was in 196, after the Wall had served to keep them out for sixty years.

Four years later the new emperor Septimus Severus restored and strengthened the Wall and regarrisoned it with fresh troops. From time to time after that, troops were withdrawn again and, despite a permanent cavalry patrol north of the Wall, the Picts broke through. But not disastrously and the Wall did its job until A.D. 383 when the garrison was withdrawn to defend Rome herself against hordes of barbarians more terrible than the tribesmen from Scotland.

This wall, one of the most substantial marks which the Romans left on England's face, was not the only one in Britain; but the other was built in Scotland. It was the Antonine wall, an earthwork joining the firths of Clyde and Forth, and after it was built following the emperor Hadrian's death in 138, Hadrian's Wall was, for a time, left only lightly garrisoned. But the attempt to create a Caledonian province was soon abandoned, and Hadrian's Wall again became the last frontier.

So, to the wilderness of England and Wales, but not Scotland, the Romans added towns, roads and the Wall. But these were not their only marks, and other changes were wrought on the land's face before the end of their epoch. First, there were the villas. It is not absolutely true

Left: *bronze head found in the Thames at London Bridge. It is a portrait of the Emperor Hadrian.* Right: *The Corbridge Lion.*

to say that Scotland's face was unmarked by Rome: the multiple ditches which protected the fort at Ardoch in Perthshire are still to be seen; tombstones and altars remain to bear testimony to the manning of the Scottish or Antonine Wall; but there were no Roman roads, villas or towns in Scotland.

Roman officials and military officers, and the richer British – Latinized tribal aristocrats, rich merchants and the wealthier farmers – built themselves villas on the Roman model; this pattern of living as a country gentleman with all the refinements of urban civilization was to be an enduring one – that of the big country house surrounded by a formal garden and beyond that by a park and home farms.

The word *villa* in Latin means a farm: what was actually designated in the times we are concerned with was a big establishment based on agriculture but including a certain amount of industry: for, attached to the estate, were craftsmen – smiths, carpenters, workers in local specialities – who made things not only for the estate, but for sale. The house itself, at least in England, had foundations of local stone and a half-timbered, single-storey structure on those foundations, the material being whatever the locality afforded. The roof was made of clay daub on a wattle base carried by timbering, and then tiled or slated. The inside of the daub was plastered and either whitewashed or painted. The floors were mosaic. They were either abstract designs in bright colours, or mosaic pictures representing heroes of mythology or minor gods, animals, signs of the zodiac and so forth. In fact, they were very like carpets to look at. The houses were centrally heated in the manner described by Gerald the Welshman, and every one had a suite of baths. There were several different basic designs: there were simple cottages, a passage with one or more rooms on either side; the winged corridor house, with a veranda along the front of the main building and rooms projecting at either end; the courtyard house, that is a house built round a central courtyard, and, as a rule, very large; and the aisled house, a house based on the nave-with-aisles plan, also usually large. There are some deviations from these four plans, but they are few and not very important.

We know of some 500 such villas and it is certain that there were many more whose sites will be discovered, or are for ever lost under our own buildings. The farms serving some might be small, but it is also known that many were large, and might well extend to a thousand acres or perhaps more. So that villa-building with its associated open-field cultivation, in contrast to the fenced-field cultivation round the tribal villages, must, even if there were no more than a thousand villas in all England and Wales, have made a considerable mark on the face of the land, and did go a little way towards transforming a wild land into a man-made one.

Formal gardens appeared in England for the first time, with both rectangular and serpentine walks planted with evergreens – probably box; with bowers, statues, fountains and fruit-trees; and perhaps a few flowers. At this time were introduced some of the weeds of our wayside, things we think of as native but which were introduced by Roman gardeners – valerian, for example. This made a small change in the permanent wild flora. A larger change was made in the cultivated flora: Roman gardeners failed to establish the olive tree, but the grape-vine and the fig flourished and the first vineyards were planted about 280; not earlier, because the Italian wine exporters had persuaded the Imperial government to impose a ban on planting new vineyards outside Italy which was not lifted until then. The first cultivated cherries reached Britain at this time, then peaches, some plums, improved kinds of apples and pears and a number of herbs including rosemary. I think, too, that the Romans may have brought some of their favourite trees, planes, poplars and perhaps the cypress.

Did these new plants survive the collapse of Roman civilization in Britain, or were they reintroduced much later? Some certainly did survive; Bede, for example, writing in the eighth century, speaks of grape-vines as being one of England's cultivated plants.

Above: *view of Hadrian's Wall near Housesteads in Northumberland.*

Left: *figure of the Celtic god Taranis from a pottery mould, found at Corbridge Roman station, Northumberland.*

Below: *Hadrian's Wall, guarding civilized Roman Britain from the savage, tribal north.*

Long before the final withdrawal of the Roman legions from England, the towns were running down and even decaying. This does not mean that all of them disappeared. Many became the nucleus of later towns, perhaps after a long period of semi-existence as half-ruined villages. Roman civilization lasted much longer in the villas, however; men retreated to their country houses and there held out, defending the literate, civilized way of life until the last against the advancing tide of barbarism.

Another way in which the Romans altered the face of England, if not the rest of Britain, was in the beginnings of land-drainage. A vast area of Lincolnshire and Cambridgeshire was once fen; to see what it was like now you have to visit Wicken Fen where the National Trust carefully maintains a piece of England in that primeval condition. The Roman engineers started the long job of digging dikes and drainage canals, and building causeways, which made the rich silts farmable, and in consequence that part of England became more populated with native villages. The Car Dyke is a surviving example of Roman work here, and the Foss Dyke is another. So there was some transformation in the look of England in East Anglia.

It is important, at this point, to warn against the feeling that the Romans and Romano-Britons somehow transformed all Britain from a land of primeval forests and open grasslands, of fens and savage mountains, inhabited by wild beasts and a few savages who, though gifted artists in metal, were still technologically backward, into a civilized man-shaped land. This is very far from being the case. At a generous estimate there may have been seventy or eighty Roman towns but most of them did not exceed twenty acres in extent within the walls, although some no doubt had extramural suburbs – in fact they must have had. It has been estimated that there may have been as many as 2,500 rural settlements of one kind or another, that is villas with their farms, native villages with their surrounding cultivation on which the people lived. It has also been estimated that 300 acres per settlement would be a very high guess at the average of land under cultivation or permanent pasture. In short, if, in Roman times, as much as two per cent of what we have now claimed from the wild had already been so claimed, that is certainly as much as it can possibly have been. And it was not even permanent: a lot of the reclaimed farmland went back to marsh in the ensuing centuries.

The Roman roads cut through the ancient wilderness of England but they did not radiate Latin civilization outwards from all along their

Above: *The hygienic and practical Romans constructed very efficient latrines even in their northern outpost.*

Left: *Doorway of the Roman fort at Chesters along Hadrian's Wall.*

Below: *a geometric panel from a mosaic floor in Lullingstone Roman villa.*

Above: *the Triple dyke, Lexden Straight Road.* Below: *a section of the Sheepen dyke revealed in a gravel pit.*

The Roman bridge, still standing, at Castle Combe.

length. They linked town to town, settlement to settlement, but these points were tiny clearances in the wilderness, hardly more than seeds of civilization. In their vicinity there were changes in England's face, but neither the Roman plough nor the Roman will were stout enough to set about transforming Britain from a province of nature into a province of man.

If you walk or drive along any road in England today you are aware that the whole land on either side of you is under our control and is serving one of our purposes. If your drive happens to be through one of the small remaining areas of wild country which is neither built on nor cultivated, you are aware that, just beyond it, cultivation and building begin again. The road does not isolate you from the country, it takes you into it. But walking or riding a Roman road you would have known yourself in country alien and hostile to man, and for the most part untouched by him. You can – just – still manage to have this experience in our world: I have known it myself, driving from one town to another in Brazil.

In short, the Romans did begin the taming of Britain; but they did not make much impression on it.

4 The Saxon Clearances

According to the great historian of the Old English, the Venerable Bede, in his *Ecclesiastical History of the English Nation*, the English originated in three German peoples, the Angles, the Saxons and the Jutes. Modern authorities tend to agree that this was so but that no distinction need be made between these three elements, and we can do as Alfred the Great did in his own writings and call them all English. From what Bede says about the length of time the English had been in England at the time of his writing, it has been calculated that they first began to settle in England in the year 449, at the invitation of their ally, the Romano-British King Vortigern. What we know for sure is that they began to take an interest in this country in the third century, first as pirates raiding the east coast and against whom the Romans had to build and man special coast defences and a fleet; that they did begin to settle here in the middle of the fifth century; and that they did so at first by treaty, and only later by conquest.

From the fifth century to the eleventh they kept coming, pushing farther and farther west until they held the whole country short of Wales and the north and west of Scotland. This does not mean that they killed off all the Celts, of course. The Celtic element remained, as did the still older ones.

I said in the last chapter that at the end of the Roman occupation most of England remained as untouched by man as it had been when the ice of the last glaciation retreated and the great deciduous forests spread across all Europe including England, Wales and southern Scotland, in the wake of the conifers, as the climate warmed up. At least ninety-eight of every hundred acres of land which is now either farmland, or is built on, was still in a state of nature in the fifth century. The forests of Selwood, Wychwood, Savernake, Wyre, Arden, Sherwood, Epping, Kinver, Morfe and the Chilterns were dark, continuous woodlands, vastly more extensive than they are now, and in which the voice of man had scarcely been heard since the time of the Mesolithic hunters came to

The Alfred Jewel, found at Atholmoy in Somerset in 1693. It is inscribed in Anglo-Saxon: 'Alfred had me made'.

an end. From Kent to Hampshire the Weald was unbroken forest, a great army of trees 120 miles long and thirty miles broad. In Sussex, Somerset and Lincolnshire and neighbouring counties there were enormous expanses of marsh and fen with huge populations of wild fowl and wading birds. The Scottish and Welsh highlands were virtually untouched.

The light network of Roman civilization which had been laid across this wilderness had now fallen apart and was decaying; the towns were deserted, the roads beginning to be overgrown; only some of the villas survived in use; and, of course, the Belgic settlements and villages.

The incoming English occupied hardly any of the Roman towns, although they were enormously impressed by them. They were not accustomed to live in cities; builders in wood, lath and plaster, they had no stonemasons or bricklayers to repair the Roman houses. They could have employed Britons to do it for them, but they were not interested in city life. Nor, at first, did they have much use for roads. In some places they did build villages which in due course grew into towns, in the same places as their predecessors; but always beside the older foundation, never on exactly the same site. And there were many other ways in which the English seemed determined to have nothing to do with the natives of the land they were colonizing: they were not converted to Christianity by the Christian Romano-Britons, but only later, the south of the island by the Augustine mission from Rome, and the north by the Irishman, Aidan's, special mission from Iona; they borrowed very few Celtic or Latin words; and, what is more to the point, they did not, as a rule, take over existing high-land farms or villages, even when they defeated the Celts in war, preferring to break new country. In short, they were tough German heathen, fanatically loyal to their warlords to whom, in return for service, they looked for their horses, weapons and food, but for the rest men who liked to be free and masters in their own houses.

The most important changes made by these Old English on the face of England were of two kinds: in the clearing of forest and the bringing of heavy clay soils under the plough; and in the building of villages. It was they who established the pattern of villages so distinctive of England; nearly every village which exists in England today was an Anglo-Saxon creation.

The use of 'England' rather than 'Britain' in the paragraph above is deliberate: although it is no longer possible to credit the Victorian historians' vision of the whole British people fleeing west and north to take refuge in the hill country, leaving the rest of the island, that is England, empty for the Saxon occupation, there is at least something in it. Wales remained a pre-Celtic and Celtic stronghold throughout the Saxon dominion, so much so that in the decade before the Norman Conquest the Godwinsons and Leofricsons who between them ruled England during the latter part of Edward the Confessor's reign had still to treat with the Welsh princes as with allies or enemies on an equal footing. As for Scotland, Saxon penetration of the lowlands was slow, while the highlands retained their integrity into the eighteenth century. It had, after all, been an alliance, if only a tacit one, between the Anglo-Saxon invaders from the east and the Picto-Scottish invaders from the north, which overcame British resistance in England.

It used to be thought that the Old English brought with them from Germany a plough which was more massive and in general better than the Roman and Celtic ploughs, and that it was this which enabled them to plough up the heavy lowland soils neglected by their predecessors. This theory has now been abandoned, for it seems that their ox-drawn wheeled plough was not substantially different from the one used by the Belgic tribes. Instead, we have to conclude that it was Saxon energy, Saxon will and perhaps the pressure of increasing population which drove the immigrants to tackle the job of felling forests and claiming difficult soils for cultivation. In due course, there was another factor: very considerable areas of good land were pre-empted by their great men, the thanes, who held many great estates, so that poorer men may have been driven by necessity as much as anything else to undertake the more difficult kinds of clearance.

The new look which the Saxons began to impose upon England and south-west Scotland by the founding of villages was not simply a matter of buildings, streets or rectangles of small wooden houses, but also of the cultivated land which surrounded each village and which the villagers lived on. This was the real beginning of what is called 'open-field' cultivation. Each village brought one, two or three big fields into cultivation. Each farmer – that is, each head of a household – had a certain number of strips in this big field. In theory a strip should have been 220 yards long and twenty-two yards wide, that is, one acre; in practice it is clear that strips were much more commonly only half or even one third of an acre, so that as far as possible each man had a share of both the best and worst land in the field. Strips were grouped in units called *cultura* or, in English, *furlongs*. There were scores of these furlongs to a big field, so that each open field contained several hundred strips.

Anglo-Saxons working in the fields scything and harvesting the grain; from the Luttrel Psalter.

Ploughing was always done the long way of the strip, first up and then down; and as the plough turned the soil inwards towards the centre of the strip, each strip became a ridge, the sort of thing you can see in well-tended French kitchen-gardens. Each of these strips was separated from its neighbours either by a balk of unploughed land or by a double furrow.

The earliest of these open fields were made along the banks of rivers, for the immigrants came in boats and set about the work of making settlements when they came to a place which seemed suitable. There must have been anxious months, at first, with great anxiety as to whether any stores they had brought with them would last, with the help of some hunting and fishing, until the first harvest. They would begin with making an arable field just large enough for their number; pigs and cattle, under the guard of the elderly, the boys and their dogs, would be allowed to find a living for themselves in the woods. Then, year after year, as the settlement grew, the area under cultivation would

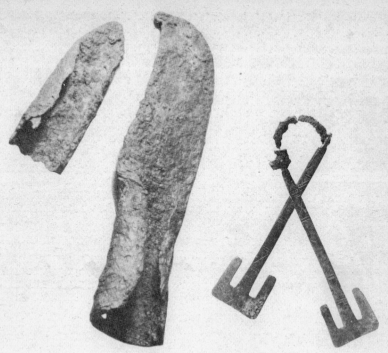

The iron tip of a Belgic plough, and a billhook, from Caburn, Sussex, and right: 'girdle hangers' from an Anglo-Saxon cemetery at Morton, Cambridgeshire.

be increased by more tree-felling and grubbing, the burning off of scrub, the clearing and ploughing of rough grassland. Little by little the forest gave way, replaced by an immense patchwork quilt done in greens and browns, reds and whites, laid down over the land.

It was not, of course, continuous. We, with our bulldozers and motor-shovels, motor-saws, tractors, immensely powerful machine ploughs, can have very little idea of the slowness imposed on our ancestors in their work of remaking England by the fact that they had only their own muscles and those of their animals to do their work with.

The extent of the new patchwork pattern varied from one part of England to another: in the east midlands, where villages were not more than a mile or two apart, the field pattern began to dominate the land; in the south-west, villages were more scattered, five or six miles apart, and the new pattern was not only discontinuous, but variegated by the survival of Celtic settlements of fenced and hedged fields round small groups or clusters of houses.

The pattern of ancient fields shows through in this aerial photograph of the modern (left) layout of fields.

The achievement of the Old English in changing the face of Britain during the first five centuries of their settlement was much greater than that of all the peoples who came before them. When they arrived, for example, the whole of the midlands was still continuous primeval forest which none of the earlier farmers had touched. By Bede's day, in the eighth century, this had become the rich and powerful kingdom of Mercia, with villages, hamlets and isolated farms, and noblemen's estates, where there had been nothing but trees, deer and wolves.

In some parts of Britain, especially in England, the open-field patchwork pattern gave way earlier to the enclosed, hedged fields of various shapes and sizes which is a pattern much more familiar to us than that of the open field: in Kent, Essex, Lancashire and Devonshire this change occurred long before it happened elsewhere. Why this was so, and exactly when it happened, are two things which have not yet been explained; but it is a fact that, when enclosures first began in Tudor times, the enclosure of agricultural land in those four counties, and in one or two other places, was already so ancient that it was assumed that open-field agriculture had never been practised there. Aerial photo-

Shenington, Oxfordshire, an aerial view of Saxon strip-lynchets and cultivation terraces.

graphy, with its extraordinary power to reveal the shape of the past just below the surface, has made it clear that this was not so. Certainly the open-field system was practised all over Saxon Britain from the fifth to the eleventh centuries, and that this was not changed but intensified by the Danish conquest of the north.

If the principal change made in the look of Britain by the Old English was the covering of regions of the country with villages and open-field farms, it was not the only one. There were a number – nobody seems to know how many – of isolated farmsteads with fenced farms. These were commoner in the south-west than anywhere in the east of the country, and they seem usually to have been made in forest clearings which were slowly enlarged, like those of the village communities. It seems as if these must have been the work of individualists willing, for the sake of being lords of all they surveyed, to take the risk of living alone with their families. We are familiar with this type in the history of the settlement of North America. Trees were felled with the axe; scrub cleared with the billhook; roots broken out with the mattock. I once cleared a couple of acres of rough land myself with precisely those tools, and without the help of any machine: and very rough, hard, slow work it was, but satisfying! Then, as with their Neolithic predecessors, there is evidence that the Old English used fire to clear land. Sometimes the fire got out of hand; there are some Anglo-Saxon law codes which provide for fines to be paid to a neighbour whose trees one had inadvertently set fire to.

I doubt very much whether the burning out of clearings was a common practice, though. Timber was much too valuable; not, of course, because there was any want of trees, but because of the labour of felling them. If trees were felled with the axe, you were both enlarging your clearing and providing yourself with building material, the material for making tools and implements and furniture, and, of course, fuel.

This two-birds-with-one-stone policy was applied in another way, too. I have already mentioned the practice of running herds of pigs, and even of cattle, in the woods. The farm animals which got their living off the forest floor were not only supporting themselves at very little cost in labour to the farmer, they were also helping him to clear land. In the history of animal domestication it is an interesting fact that whereas, in the Neolithic Middle East, goats took priority over sheep on wooded land, sheep took priority over goats on open grassy parkland. Where you had such open land, sheep were more profitable. But if your land was heavily wooded and had to be cleared for the plough, then goats were better; they are browsers, living on foliage rather than grass; they 'bark', and thus kill, trees; and they eat seedling trees. The first domesticated goats were just as valuable for their work as woodland destroyers, as for their meat and skins. The pattern was the same in Britain thousands of years later: the Saxon's swine ate up the acorns which would otherwise have grown into trees, and rooted up tree seedlings, thus preventing natural regeneration of the trees. Even cows set to graze in the woods will eat seedling trees and sprouting brambles in the youthful soft stage, and help to clear the undergrowth. All of which made the axeman's task easier when the time came to fell that piece of the forest.

Before the tenth century, the Old English had established all of the several varieties of villages which are characteristic of the English, and parts of the Welsh and Scottish, countryside. In the lowlands, the village built round a green was the rule. This green was common land, and the people whose houses fronted it had grazing rights for some cattle and for geese. The only buildings allowed on the green were the church, the smithy and, later, when there were such things, the school. As a rule, the village well was sunk on the green. At the backs of the houses which surrounded the green were farm-buildings for

Aerial view of Laxton fields in Nottinghamshire which shows the beautiful pattern of cultivated fields which still exist over much of the face of England.

housing animals, tools and carts, linked by a ring-road from which roads led away to the big fields and to any main road which connected the village to other communities. These were often the old Roman roads, so that all over England and into north and south Wales stretches of these roads began to be taken back into use, and more or less repaired and maintained. Probably the earliest of these green villages, as they are called, were also surrounded by a wooden fence or stockade, to make the place easily defensible against wolves, and perhaps, also, against raiding human beings; for even when the governments of the Heptarchy, the seven kingdoms which emerged in Old England – Kent, Sussex, Wessex, East Anglia, Essex, Northumbria and Mercia – were more or less firmly established, they were not such strong central governments as could ensure peaceful farmers against bands of landless, lawless men.

Then there were the single-street villages we are also still familiar with, the oldest of which date from (at latest) the eighth century. No-

Finchingfield, Essex. One of the most beautiful of English villages, built up very much on the hugger-mugger principle of streets rising up a small incline, with the church at the top and a lovely green and pond below with houses and shops encircling it. The name means 'The Field of Finc's People', and it was obviously well established as a village in Saxon times.

body seems to know why some villages were built round a green or, as in the west country, round a square which might, later, be paved; others in a single, long street; and yet others hugger-mugger. I suppose that the street village might, in the very early cases, have been a product of the local topography; it would be difficult to build a square village in a steep-sided valley and it is in such valleys that many street villages survive; later street villages were those which came into existence as two rows of houses on an old main road, with the open fields behind them on both sides. This would have been a matter of convenience.

As for the hugger-mugger villages, surely they must have come into existence in much the same way as the similar small towns of the people who opened up North America. A number of individual settlers, not originally bound together as a community, but settling near to each other for the sake of company and security, each cleared his own bit of land, each built his house, however it suited him, so that there was no plan, no regularity of any kind. Naturally, these people visited each

Long Melford, Suffolk. A good example of the village built round an extensive green with all the houses, churches, shops and pubs along the edges.

other, had a social life, business to transact together; so a network of paths, gradually turning into tracks and at last into roads, joined the houses into one village.

In order to explain other changes wrought in the look of England and the Scottish region of Strathclyde by the Old English, it is necessary to say a little about the class-structure of Anglo-Saxon society. The sort of people we have been talking about, the village builders and land-clearers, were churls, that is to say freemen of the lowest class. Class distinctions were marked by *wergild*. If you killed a man, the compensatory fine you had to pay his family, the blood-money, was called *wergild*. Allowing for variations due to local custom or to different values of the shilling (from as low as 4 pence in Mercia to as high as 20 pence in Kent), a churl's *wergild* was about 200 shillings. Above the churls was a class of petty nobles or gentry whose *wergild* was 600 shillings. These were men who held at least five hides (about 600 acres) of land. Above

A 'street' village. This is Old Oxted in Surrey.

these six hundreders was the class of twelve hundred men, first known as ealdormen, later as thanes, except in Kent where they were called earls.

The thanes held more or less large estates, some of them very large indeed, and not one each, but many. I should add, in justice to our ancestors, that a churl could become a thane if he prospered sufficiently to hold the qualifying acreage of land; and that if a churl's *wergild* was lower, so too were the fines he had to pay in the event of being convicted of a crime or misdemeanour: for example, in the time of Alfred the Great, a thane who failed to report for duty when summoned to do his military service was fined 120 shillings; a churl only 30 shillings.

The point is that, as well as the village and farmstead cleared lands, there were the great estates of the thanes, setting a pattern as enduring as that of the village: the great country house, with its home farms, is still very much a feature of Britain, particularly England. There were Saxon noblemen who owned ten, twenty, even seventy such estates, in return for military service due to the king as representative of the people, service which included arming, feeding and sometimes even

A flat, unbroken, wild-seeming place; Romney Marsh in Kent.

mounting from ten to several hundred churls called to the colours; and for some other public services, such as bridge-building and maintenance, and care of roads. Of course, these estates were not by any means all cleared of wilderness to be turned into farmlands. Much of their territory might simply be used as a hunting park. But every great hall-house belonging to a thane had its home farm, so that such estates also changed parts of the land's face, with their ploughed fields, their orchards, farm buildings and cottages.

Despite the fact that in the ninth century the Danes began to try to seize lands, they did contribute to the task of turning the great forest, marsh and moor into a land fit for civilized people to live in. This did not differ from the change wrought by the English themselves. Danish soldier-adventurers engaged to serve their warlords for a certain term in exchange for a promise of part of what they conquered. So, when their term of service was completed, they sent for their families and settled down to transform the piece of country they had been awarded into a farmstead. A great deal of northern England, even in the north-east, and

Lingfield in Surrey. A medieval by-way leading to the parish church containing some of the finest old houses in the village. The half-timbered building on the left is early sixteenth century; built as a shop, it has remained one ever since. The church, dedicated to St Peter and St Paul, has a long association with one of the great families in English history, the Cobhams of Steerborough, whose tombs and effigies for seven generations are to be found within.

even more of Wales and Scotland, was still virgin land. So that what this Danish incursion did was simply to add to the number of people busy clearing forest and draining marsh.

Like the English, the Danes built villages based on open-field agriculture. Whether Danish villages differed from English ones is hard to say. No such differences can now be detected. But 1,000 years may have obliterated ancient distinctions. What matters to us is only that village building, and all it implied, was increased as a result of the Danish conquest.

The Danes did one thing which the Saxons seem not to have done: they resumed the drainage of the eastern fens, first undertaken by the Romans, digging drainage channels and dikes. There were Danish settlements in this wet country composed of a number of small independent farmsteads clustered round a tiny hamlet. It is not quite true to say that the Old English had done nothing about such marshlands; but certainly the Danes were more active in the work. They established a fen country way of life which did not just entail accepting the conditions and living on eel fishing and such fenland occupations. Instead, they transformed small areas into farmland, beginning that encroachment into the domain of the tall wading birds, the wildfowl and the otters which has ended, in our own day, in the need to preserve, at great trouble and expense, what little remains of this kind of country.

At the end of the period of English and Danish settlement the population of Britain had risen to about 1,500,000 people. This is only a rough estimate, but it cannot be very far from the true figure. The most populous counties were Norfolk, Lincolnshire and Suffolk. Devonshire probably had about 70,000 people in all its vast extent. The Yorkshire population is hard to estimate because the only figures we have are based on Domesday Book entries and, as the Domesday survey was made two decades after the Norman conquest, in which Yorkshire was devastated, the estimate of under 30,000 is certainly misleading. The south-east, Kent, Sussex and Hampshire, now by far the most congested region of England if one includes London, probably had about 150,000 people. The least populous counties had about four people to the square mile; the most populous, about forty.

The look of England and parts of Scotland and Wales just before the Norman Conquest had been greatly changed since A.D. 450, by the clearance of woods, the draining of marshes and the advance of the farmers on to the high, stony moorlands such as Dartmoor; by the increase in the mining of iron and copper; by the building of villages all over the country; by the reoccupation of a few Roman towns like London and Bristol; by the building of churches, especially in the south-east, of stone, mostly by imported Norman builders and perhaps one or two Italians. But by far the greater part of Britain was still in a state of nature. The entire population of the country was not so large as the number of people who, today, commute between their homes in the suburbs and the working centre of London.

The primeval forest was still predominant. Great tracts of land which are now under cultivation or under masonry were still waterlogged, given over to wading birds and other creatures of the wild. Seen from the air great tracts of Britain would still have looked like a province of nature, a land of endless treetops broken only by the glint of waters and the hill and moor country barriers, scarcely touched by man.

Two beautiful and picturesque watermills. Above: the watermill at Cobham. Below: the old watermill at Rossett, Denbighshire, in North Wales, one of the oldest water-mills anywhere in Great Britain.

But there was a portent in that scene: machines had made their first appearance. The first water-mill had appeared in England in the eighth century and at the time of the Conquest in the eleventh century there were, according to Domesday Book, 6,000 such mills. Since that survey can hardly have been complete, there were doubtless more than that. Even in Britain, that far western outpost of Eurasian civilization, man was no longer utterly dependent on his own muscles; at least his corn was being ground into flour by water power.

5 Deforestation and Building

When the Domesday Book survey was made in 1086 the village communities of England were like small colonial settlements of a few hundred stockaded acres, islanded in a land of primeval forest, marsh and moor. We tend to picture the old England as an emptier, cleaner version of our own rural England; but it was not. Its aspect was quite different; like most of Wales and Scotland, it was a jungle, if one may use the word in a temperate-zone context, in which settlement, although not new, had not yet 'taken' very well.

As well as the villages there were a few little towns, some of these built on the sites of the old Roman towns, others inflated villages. But the number was astonishingly small, and so was their size: only five towns in all Anglo-Saxon England had more than 1,000 households – London, Norwich, Lincoln, Winchester and York, and most towns had only between one and two score burgesses – a burgess was a citizen head-of-household. The majority of towns we think of as having always been there – for although we know that man-made things which are ancient in the landscape were once new, we do not *feel* it to be so – were not even founded; and their sites were still forest, marsh or moorland, the haunt of deer and boar, wolf and bear, fox and marten, wildfowl and wader.

For every thirty-six Englishmen, Scots and Welshmen alive today, there was then only one. But there was not, and for centuries to come would not be, nearly enough people to make proper use of the land: it was a case of too much material for too few craftsmen and labourers.

On the clay soils oak, ash and elm were as yet very much more numerous than people; they, not men, were still masters of the greater part of England, as were pines of the Scottish highlands. On soils at higher altitudes, which overlay the limestones, the beech, a relative newcomer, had colonized many hundreds of square miles, and there were more hundreds of square miles of thin birch woodlands on the sandy soils. On the other hand, scores of tree species which for us are very much part of the country scene, were absent: there were not only no pines but no firs, spruces, cedars, sycamores, holm-oaks, planes, chestnuts ... except one or two ancient specimens of the last two species surviving from the fourth century.

So the principal task which faced the English under the Normans and the Scots and Welsh under Norman influence, was very much the same as it had been under their own princes: to breed the people to clear the trees and drain the marshes so that Britain could be used as the more ancient lands of the East had long been used, to make 'the good life', the life of urban sophistication, for men and women. Today large families are frowned upon as contrary to the interests of our own over-crowded race; in those days a man and woman could best enrich their country by helping to people it.

Meanwhile the forest verges which still crowded in and loomed darkly over the villages were being steadily forced back by felling and new clearings, and new villages on all three Anglo-Saxon models were being founded.

Suppose that you had a film shot with a movie camera mounted on the platform of a satellite in orbit high above any of the great forest regions of Britain, a film which had been exposed at the rate of one frame every midsummer day every year for 500 years from 1066 to 1566; and that you projected it on to a screen. At first you would see a great expanse of green fabric – treetops – with little rents or holes in it, few and small to begin with, growing steadily larger as the film progressed, and more numerous too. As the rents enlarged they would join to make large holes, and meanwhile, at the edges, the green foliage fabric would be contracting towards the middle of the picture, not in a regular shrinking, but irregularly, in capes and bays, like the map of a coast. At last there would be more hole than fabric, the fabric would be seen reduced to a ragged vestige, with some large pieces still, and many small pieces islanded by the process of clearance all round them. As for the great clearance now occupying most of the picture, part of it would appear as the familiar patchwork pattern of the open field, part of it as a reticulated pattern of hedges round irregular fields, the hedges looking like threads connecting the rags and tatters of remaining woodland.

Such was the transformation wrought by countrymen between the Norman conquest and Tudor times. At its beginnings it must have seemed that no effort made by a few hundred thousand men could ever

The Norman Conquest had many influences upon the English countryside, reflected strongly in its architecture, with the introduction of the beautiful rounded Norman arch. The one pictured above is on the West Door of the Norman church at Barfreston, Kent. The ancient name means 'Beornrith's Farm'.

make more than a marginal impression on the trees, although one reads of foresters who, in a lifetime, single-handed felled 30,000 oaks. And such men were the true portents, not the apparently overwhelming number of the trees; for such was their energy that by Tudor times industry in England was growing seriously short of timber for house-building and ship-building and men of vision were not felling oaks but planting them.

The slow and mighty work did not go steadily forward unchecked for five centuries. It suffered setbacks of several kinds, not the least being the vicious Norman Game Laws. Under the native English kings – Harold Godwinson was the last Englishman ever to be king of England – the king and the great thanes did, indeed, have their hunting parks, lineal descendants of the hunting parks of the aristocracies in the ancient Asian civilizations, and ancestors of the country gentleman's deer park. They were fenced or enclosed by banks, and poaching or trespass inside these enclosures was an offence punishable by a fine and, in practice as I suspect, by a beating from the thane's servants. But all men were free to hunt and make clearings outside the limits of such parks.

But the Norman forest law imposed after the Conquest was ferocious. Under it, enormous tracts of England were designated Royal Forest (the word 'forest' was used in the sense still familiar in Scotland and did not imply the presence of trees); and savage punishments, including mutila-tion, were provided for any man caught killing game within the royal forest, heavy fines for any man felling trees or in any way disturbing the land, for example, in prospecting for minerals. Hundreds of villages were, of course, within regions denominated Royal Forest, so that tens of thousands of people were under these restraints even in their own parish. The Welsh under their own princes in their fastnesses, and the Scots still under kings of their own race, kept their own laws for a little longer; but King Malcolm III of Scotland, the one who with the help of Saxon and Dane overthrew the usurper Macbeth, and whose reign covered that of both William the Conqueror and William Rufus, did not merely 'anglicize' the lowlands – his wife, Margaret, was an Englishwoman – but 'normanized' them.

The practice began with William the Conqueror himself; his turning of a rich area of farmland and villages back into wilderness – the New Forest – is notorious. Later the whole county of Essex, and a vast area of the midlands from Stamford Bridge to Oxford Bridge became Royal Forest. Then there was another great tract of land, from Windsor to the coast of Hampshire. By the middle of Henry II's reign one third of all

England was under Forest Law. Happily this did not always or often mean that villages were razed and farmland returned to the wild, as it had done in the New Forest. It did mean that the clearing of forest and the draining of marshes to create new agricultural land or pasture was checked; that farmers had to endure the breaking down of their fences and the spoiling of their crops by deer and rabbits, and noble huntsmen riding over their corn. It is little wonder that William II died of a Saxon hunting arrow.

However, the system of fines for making new clearances or for prospecting on land under Forest Law evolved into a sort of fines-paid-in-advance arrangement: the peasants would club together to pay the king a large lump sum for the deforestation of their land. The land was theirs, yet they had to buy it back; but they were realists and knew they could not fight their Norman masters. Devonshire farmers, for example, paid King John 5,000 marks – say half a million sterling of our money – to have their county, except Dartmoor and Exmoor, freed from Forest Law. By this means clearance, draining and prospecting could go forward again.

Another and far more terrible check to the progress of the work of changing Britain's face was the Black Death. But before we come to that we should look at one or two other ways in which that work was being pushed forward. There was, for example, the work of the prospectors and miners already mentioned, of the industrialists who fore-ran the industrial age.

For many centuries salt had been procured from the operation of salt-pans on the coasts, and in the salt-bearing districts of Cheshire and Worcestershire. The earliest known charter referring to this industry is one granted by King Aethelbald to the diocese of Worcester in 716; and by 1086 there were 285 salt-pans in, for example, the county of Sussex alone; some thousands, therefore, in the whole country.[1] For this industry furnaces had to be built – and fuelled, which meant more tree-felling – and salt-houses erected; and their number naturally increased with the growth of population. A prosperous industry generates a prosperous trade; Droitwich became the centre of that trade, so the growth and wealth of that borough was founded on salt.

The iron industry was even more effective in changing England's face, although its great development belongs to a later chapter. Its

[1] D. Whitelock, *The Beginnings of English Society*. Harmondsworth, 1952.

The so-called New Forest. An area of rich farming land and villages which William the Conqueror turned back into wilderness, reversing the trend previously established.

Above: *a section of the famous Bayeux tapestry. It shows the scene before the Conquest when William and Harold, not yet king, met at Bayeux and Harold swore an oath of allegiance to William. He then returned to England, where he heard of King Edward's death and his own election to the throne. The news was brought to Duke William and he began to marshal the great invasion force which so changed the history of England.*

Below: *again from the Bayeux tapestry, a depiction of Westminster Abbey, the final resting place of Edward the Confessor.*

origins were prehistoric, it grew steadily throughout the Anglo-Saxon period, and more quickly following the Conquest. One of its side-effects was forest clearance because iron-smelting was done with charcoal, as was all the smith's work; as a result, very large numbers of oaks were felled to make charcoal. Iron was worked in Kent and Sussex, in Northamptonshire, Lincolnshire and Yorkshire, and above all in the forest of Dean.

Coal in small quantities was used by the Romans, by the Romano-Britons and by the Saxons. Mined in Durham and on Tyneside, it was shipped south to London before and after the Conquest. But until the invention of coke for smelting, its use was limited and coal-mining made only insignificant local scars on the land's face. The same is true of other kinds of mining: in the west country there was a boom in tin-mining late in the twelfth century, promoted by Jewish merchants. Lead had been mined, notably in Derbyshire, since the eighth century, and as the demand for the metal increased as a result of church-building on a grand scale, so did prospecting for lead in many parts of the country and despite the constraints imposed by Forest Law.

Prospecting for minerals advanced the settlement of new country – the rough moorland and heath which had been neglected by all the immigrants who peopled Britain because of its stony and difficult nature. When minerals such as copper and tin were found in the west country moors, or coal in the north, or lead in Derbyshire, miners settled to work them, and such settlement attracted farmers who could get no better land. So that heath and moor began to be bitten into by the plough. Thus on Dartmoor, for example, there were both single, isolated farmsteads, and hamlets consisting of small groups of farmsteads.

Forest and moor were not the only kinds of land to be claimed for the plough and the village in post-Conquest England. The fen country and marshland round and below the Wash, in Kent and in Somerset, were invaded with fresh energy. The earliest settlements had been made in the seventh and eighth centuries in the fenny and marshy east midlands along the rich silt bank between fen and marsh, from Steeping to Spalding. This great bank was built higher and diked against both sea and fen; and as the population grew and more settlers came in, new banks and dikes were made to bring more land into workable condition. It was worth the great labour, for this land was very fertile. Incidentally, the ill-named 'Roman Bank' which is encountered in several places in the region about the Wash is not Roman, but much later. The oldest of the artificial banks now carries the Wainfleet to Benington main road. I have referred to the new work done in these parts by Danish settlers – some of the villages, e.g. Skirbeck, have Danish names. But the new, twelfth-century penetration of the fens was more substantial and more sustained.

In Lincolnshire, the Saturday Dike, Hassock Dike, Asgardike and Common Dike together added fifty square miles of new arable and pasture to England between 1150 and 1200. It was kept free of flood water only by constant vigilance and labour and there are records of widespread and ruinous flooding following some neglect of the dikes.

Another way in which land was won in this quarter of England and elsewhere was by the reclamation of salt marsh formed by the tides: such marshland was embanked to keep out the sea, washed clean of salt by some seasons of fresh-water flooding, and then brought under the plough. In Lincolnshire and neighbouring counties the shape of the road network is due to the twelfth-century dike-builders, for the roads were built on top of their great banks.

Who were the enterprising people who set this kind of land-making on foot? Abbots and priors were forward in this work; so were great lay land-owners. But they were not the only ones, and such projects were often undertaken by village communities acting as co-operatives. It is too often forgotten that such communal enterprise did as much to remake the face of England as the works of rich men or institutions. Work of this kind was by no means confined to the east midlands. Hundreds of square miles were won from the Kentish marshes, such as Romney, and from the bogs of Somerset, and turned into wide, flat pastures for rapidly increasing herds of sheep.

The eleventh, twelfth and thirteenth centuries brought a very great increase in the number of buildings, in materials more lasting than timber, lath and plaster. There had, of course, been some 'Norman' stone building in England before the Norman Conquest: the first parts of Canterbury Cathedral; Edward the Confessor's Westminster Abbey; Harold Godwinson's Waltham Abbey and other abbeys and priories; Queen Margaret of Scotland's St Margaret's Chapel and her son, David the First's, Holyrood Abbey with which the king founded Edinburgh as his capital – his father, Malcolm Canmore's, had been Dunfermline. But in the three centuries following the Conquest more building of an enduring kind was done in Britain than during the thirty preceding centuries.

In the first place, there was much founding of new boroughs and

Above: *Hall Tor, Dartmoor in Devon; the wilder face of England.* Below: *another section of Romney Marshes, showing the view from one of the great silt dykes.*

building of new towns. Kings, prelates and great noblemen took a hand in this work. A few examples are worth quoting: Portsmouth was founded by Richard I in 1194; and Plymouth by the Prior of Plympton in 1250. The town which was to give birth to Shakespeare, Stratford-on-Avon, was founded and built on about a hundred acres of his demesne land by the bishop of Worcester in 1196; it was built on the geometric grid plan, each house-plot being one third of an acre. Salisbury is another twelfth-century foundation laid out on similar lines. It is of particular interest that such towns, although they later grew more or less hugger-mugger, were deliberate and planned creations, their foundations laid on land which had never been built on before. Even in a land where settled, civilized living is only as comparatively new as it is in England, it is difficult to resist the irrational sense that the old towns are as ancient, even as 'natural', as the natural features themselves. But the fact worth repeating is that in the twelfth and three subsequent centuries, Britain was still pioneer country, still a frontier.

Ludlow, Eynsham, Launceston, Newcastle-upon-Tyne and Devizes were all towns built in this deliberate way. But in a majority of cases, towns grew out of villages as a result of a countryside's demand for service industries, a market and trade. This 'organic' type of town growth accounted for several small towns in this period. It had one advantage over deliberate town-building: it was more surely enduring because it came about in response to a clear need. By no means all the newly founded, newly built towns were a success, because some of them were created by the will of some great man, dictated by pride or by the wish to be of service, in places and circumstances where there was no real call for a town.

The rise of these hundreds of small boroughs brought about another change: stretches of the old Roman roads had been restored and maintained since Saxon times when the old village-builders needed communication with neighbouring communities. Now, in addition to these fragments of the Roman road network, a new network of roads was laid on England, the Welsh lowlands and southern Scotland, roads which grew out of footpaths beaten out by the feet of men and animals going from town to town, town to village. The consolidation of such roads meant, in its turn, bridge-building or rebuilding, and many hundreds of new bridges crossed the land's rivers. And this time they were built of stone, to last for centuries.

Now, too, there was very great activity in the building of churches, great and small, for the Normans brought into England their passion for

Above: *Waltham Abbey, Essex, from the south-east.*

Below: *the south side of the chancel of Canterbury Cathedral with its Norman arched windows.*

The High Street of Salisbury in Wiltshire, seen through the battlemented gate which separates it from the Cathedral close. The history of the city began with Old Sarum, an ancient site with entrenchments. The Cathedral of the Downs was there, but its site was changed to the present Salisbury in the twelfth century and the people followed, and now only a few walls and ditches remain at Old Sarum.

the creation of beautiful buildings. By the middle of the fourteenth century there were about 550 major monastic complexes, grand priories, cathedrals, towering and lovely abbey churches like Rievaulx (1132) in Yorkshire. Every such monastic establishment meant not only grand buildings but a great expansion of agricultural clearance and pasture in the neighbourhood; and often the founding of towns.

For every priory or abbey church on the grand scale, there were at least ten parish churches built in the same epoch; some were small and modest, of rubble structure, built by communities of poor peasants; but many were magnificent works of art, built by rich lay or ecclesiastical landlords as a gift to the community. Since the tenth century, the Church had the good sense to impose building as a penance on great men seeking absolution for their sins: the Abbaye aux Hommes and the Abbaye aux Dames in Caën were built as penances by William and Matilda of Normandy – the Conqueror and his stolen wife. But some of the grandest parish churches, miniature cathedrals, were built by communities of rich peasants like those of the east midlands. Lincolnshire, Norfolk and Suffolk were very prosperous counties, where the peasants needed to look to no great man for building money, and so too was Kent. Nothing in the history of England is more remarkable and more admirable than this creation all over the land of beautiful churches by small populations. The wealth which paid for them came from wheat and, in a lesser degree, from sheep, whose great day in England was yet to come. In the thirteenth century the church steeple made its first appearance and tall spires, symbols of wealth and pride rather than piety, towered above the trees all over the land.

I have said that the marks and scars of medieval mining and industry were insignificant: they were portents, but not yet features. Water-mills and mining pits had been the chief industrial contribution to change in Anglo-Saxon times. Now, as steeples rose all over the country, so, to match them, did a newly introduced industrial building, the windmill. Windmills were built by the hundred in some counties and, taking the whole of Britain into account, there must, by the middle of the fourteenth century, have been more than 10,000 of them.

By that time, then, the face of Britain had at last been transformed, and was well on the way to being more a work of man than of nature. But the work was very far from complete. If the almost unbroken fabric of forest which had covered the country had by now been nibbled and torn

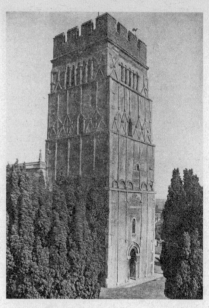

Above: *the square-towered Saxon church of Earl's Barton in Northants. The tower is seen from the north-west.* Below: *the stone bridge at Potter Heigham, a sailing centre on the Norfolk Broads.*

Above: *the west door of the church at Heath Salop*. Below: *the ruins of Rievaulx Abbey, in Yorkshire.*

into rags and tatters, even in England many of the rags were still very large, the tatters were still very numerous, and the creatures which lived in the woods were not yet being seriously persecuted and crowded out, while in the Welsh and Scottish highlands the transformation was even less manifest. The regions of land permanently waterlogged, or seasonally invaded by the sea, had shrunk very considerably because of the greed for new land of a population which was increasing much faster than ever before. Hundreds of square miles of land which, at our last review, had been under trees or water and still in a primeval state of nature, were now patterned with great cornfields and pastures, stippled with roads, dotted with villages and towns. Perhaps this was a moment when man's works and nature's were beautifully in balance.

For three centuries the growth of population and wealth had received only minor checks and setbacks. By the middle of the fourteenth century there were something like four million people in Britain, and although there was poverty and sometimes famine, the English community was rich. Then came a setback from which it took the country nearly two centuries to recover.

The appalling epidemic of that bubonic plague which became known as the Black Death struck Europe in 1346; it was brought to Russia from somewhere in Central Asia by the Tartars. It is at least possible, if not probable, that the spread westward of the disease can be connected with the movement of the Asiatic black rat, an animal which seems to have been unknown in Europe before the eleventh, perhaps even the twelfth, century. The rat is subject to the plague, and its fleas act as carriers for the plague virus. Genoese seamen carried the disease and probably diseased rats from their Crimean colony to Messina in 1347. It spread through Sicily and up Italy at a fearsome pace, reached Paris and crossed the Rhine into Germany in the autumn of 1348; a few weeks later it was killing people in England.

Nothing quite like it had been seen in post-Hellenic Europe before. People were in full health one minute, crawling home to die the next; the mortality rate generated a panic all over Europe; parents abandoned their children, priests their flocks, physicians – for what they were worth – their patients, so that many who might have recovered died rather of neglect and starvation than of the plague. By the time the pandemic phase was over and the epidemic on the decline, the population of Britain had been reduced from about four million to between two and two and a half million people; and

Windmill at Thorpeness, Suffolk.

bubonic plague was established as an endemic disease for the next five centuries.

The shrinkage of population had its effect. The impossibility of getting in the harvest in the first year and of ploughing and sowing in the second, produced a calamitous rise in food prices. That brought changes in land-holding customs, wages and, therefore, in the standing of the labouring class. It was at this time that the practice began, among landlords, of renting farms to tenant farmers who employed hired labour. More to the point, the enormous reduction in population abruptly removed the pressure on land. There was now quite enough of the best tamed land, and to spare, so that, for some decades, not only was there no point in making new clearances or draining more fens, but there was no point in remaining on difficult moorland farms, or fenland farms whose maintenance above water called for unremitting toil, when landlords were desperately looking for tenant farmers on the best lands.

So all the splendid work of the last half-century or so was abandoned; the peasants withdrew from the marginal lands. South-west Norfolk and north-west Suffolk were virtually abandoned; farmsteads fell into ruins, villages were emptied of their people, the water broke through the dikes and what had been marsh was marsh again. Nor was this desolation confined to the east midlands. In all England at least 1,300 villages and small towns were totally deserted, given back to the wilderness from which they had been won.

Another consequence of this dreadful pestilence, which changed the look of Britain and, incidentally, founded England's sixteenth-century prosperity, was the changing over of arable land into pasture for sheep. The great ecclesiastical and lay landlords, unable to get either tenants or labour to cope with the old wheat and barley economy, ruthlessly sent their remaining farmer tenants to get a living somewhere else if they could, and to starve if they could not. They then allowed the great open fields of arable to 'tumble down' to grass, and greatly increased their flocks of sheep, for sheep could be managed in thousands by a few hands.

Oddly enough, this in itself restarted the work of land reclamation from the wild. As the great sheep runs became more and more profitable with the rise of the wool trade, landlords had no reason to go back to arable farming even had they been able to get enough hands. Which meant that as the population began slowly to rise again (the rise was very slow because fourteenth-century prosperity had gone), there were landless peasants in search of subsistence farms, and rich men who saw that there was still profit in grain. Once again men began to invade the

Old Portsmouth, showing the Camber and shipping, with the twelfth-century cathedral in the background. In the cupola of the tower men used to sit and signal to the incoming ships.

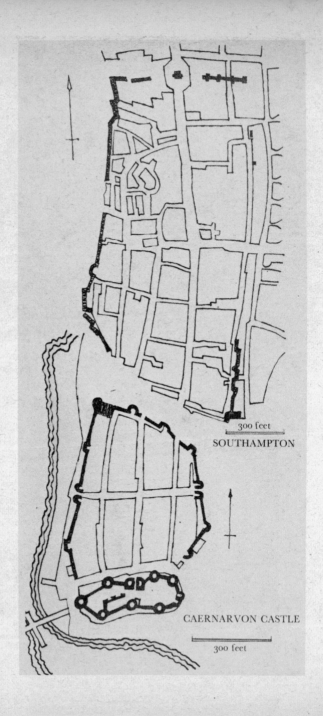

300 feet

SOUTHAMPTON

300 feet

CAERNARVON CASTLE

Above: *Launceston Castle.* Left: *Southampton town wall, twelfth to fourteenth century, and Caernarvon Castle and town wall, thirteenth and fourteenth century.* Below: *the worn steps to the entrance of Castle Rising in Norfolk.*

wild with axe and billhook, mattock and plough.

Men who, in the famine years, had made sea-fishing, from an occasional subsistence aid like hunting, into a trade as the demand for fish rose, now became professional off-shore fishermen; as a consequence, scores of new fishing villages came into being and changed the look of the coasts. Where that coast was difficult or dangerous, in Cornwall, Devon, Yorkshire, Wales, Scotland and elsewhere, men of vision with a sense of public responsibility or personal opportunity built artificial harbours of eternal granite into the sea, attracting greater populations of fishermen, and altering the inshore flow of tides so that the profiles of the coasts were changed.

We have dealt above with the deliberate building of new, planned towns in Britain. In a number of cases such towns were built as adjuncts to another kind of building which was new in England after the Norman Conquest: castles. These castles consisted of square towers built on an artificial mound made from the earth taken out by digging a moat round the site. Outside the moat was a courtyard called the bailey surrounded by a rampart of earth topped with a wooden stockade. Bailey and moat were crossed by drawbridges. Originally, in Normandy itself, such castles were built of wood, and so were some of the first in Britain. But as soon as the baron in question could afford it, he rebuilt in stone; and later the central tower – the White Tower of the Tower of London is a case in point – became more elaborate, and doubtless less uncomfortable inside. Edinburgh, Ludlow, Launceston and Devizes are also good examples. These grim stone keeps were originally built to protect the alien conquerors from the resentful conquered and to enable them to impose their will and rule from strong points which could not be stormed. In Kent alone, over forty such castles were built between 1066 and the Black Death: the density was not so great elsewhere, but hundreds were built all over Britain.

As recovery from the plague continued, there was more castle-building, although now for a different reason – each great baron was determined to be in a position to fight for his own power against the others and the kings. Then there was the enlarging, rebuilding and new building of parish churches and abbey churches: this was the age of Perpendicular Gothic. And the building of roads, bridges and mills was resumed.

Since the English wheat bonanza was over and done with, where did the wealth come from to do all this lovely work? Work so much of which

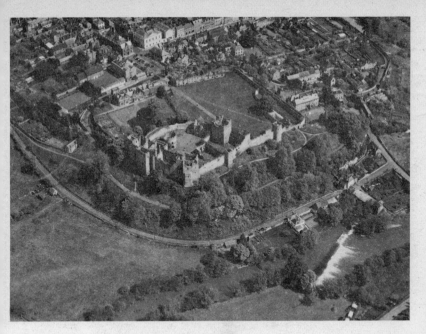

Above: *Ludlow Castle*. Below: *a plan of Ludlow, eleventh century and later*.

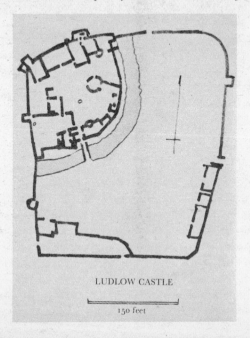

LUDLOW CASTLE

150 feet

Devizes Castle in Wiltshire.

endures and is one of the few enduring features of the look of England.
Most of it came from wool. It was a pattern which was to be repeated
half a millennium later: fifteenth-century England was the Australia of
that time. A single statistic will make the point: by the end of the
fifteenth century the human population of England and Wales, exclud-
ing Scotland, stood at something between 2.5 and three million people, a
sad falling off from the mid-fourteenth-century golden age, but still, a
recovery. It has been estimated that at the same time the sheep population of England alone was about eight million.

6   The Pattern Fills In

Until now it has been fairly easy to follow the work of remaking and of marring Britain's face, chronologically. But we may find it easier to depart from this rule now and again, advancing to modern times at one point, then at another, rather than on a broad front.

The fifteenth century had sketched on the face of Britain a thin outline of what, in the next two centuries, it would look like. It now remained to fill in the pattern with more and more detail.

Foreign visitors to this country at the opening of the sixteenth century were still surprised at the emptiness of the land and the population was still not quite up to the figure which had been attained in the decade before the Black Death. W. G. Hoskins[1] quotes an Italian tourist who was over here in about 1500 as remarking that the population appeared to bear no proportion to the riches and fertility of the island. It is difficult to be more specific for this period; not until two centuries later was there an estimate of the amount of England which had been made over out of the wild by man, of the amount of land which had been tamed and reshaped, and for the rest of Britain we have no evidence. At a guess, one can safely say that in 1500 less than one third of the country was cultivated; and that there were still at least twenty-five million acres of forest, woodland, heath, moor, marsh and untrodden mountain, lying ready to be developed but still virtually primeval. Travelling in such country could be as taxing and as dangerous as travelling today in those remote parts of the world which are still hardly explored; and from the few accounts left by travellers this was still the case more than a century later.

Taking, once again, the view from that movie camera on a satellite, the most visually striking change in the look of Britain between, say, 1500 and 1700, must have been that wrought by the last great assault on the trees.

[1] *The Making of the English Landscape*. London, 1955.

There were many destroyers of forest and woodland: builders, ship-builders, farmers making new clearances for expanding farms and, above all, perhaps, the charcoal-burners serving the iron-smelters and blacksmiths. Until coke was invented, the working of iron still demanded enormous quantities of charcoal which was made *in situ* by felling trees and burning them very slowly by smouldering, under mounds of earth. As the iron-workers' demands steadily rose, the smoke of the charcoal-burners' fires formed a thin pall, foreshadowing the industrial pall to come, over nearly every forest. By the end of the seventeenth century the forest of Arden had vanished, literally gone up in smoke, as Birmingham's iron trade grew out of it. The Kentish weald had been largely cleared of trees by the same agency, and huge new clearances had been made by the charcoal-burners all round Sheffield and in the forest of Dean.

But the charcoal-burners were only one set of men destroying the trees. As population increased, but above all as the large profits being made by the wool exporters attracted more and more land-owners, still more of the ancient forest was cleared to make way for fresh arable land and new pastures for both sheep and cattle.

Now the pattern of agricultural Britain began to vary greatly from one part of the country to another. In the north-west and south-east, the extreme north-east and in Devon and Cornwall, that patchwork pattern of the ancient open or common field was fast disappearing; in a number of places it had perhaps completely disappeared already. It was replaced by enclosures – hedged and banked fields both small and large: why this was so will presently appear. Close round these advanced regions was a zone in which about half the land was still under the common field, the other half being enclosed. Elsewhere, and notably in the midland heart of England, the manor and the common village field, with three, four or even five open fields to each village, was still dominant and hedges had scarcely made their first appearance.

Why this difference? It was made clear in an earlier chapter that in many outlying parts of England, as well as Scotland and Wales, where the first pioneering clearances were made by adventurous individuals, there never were any open-field villages, but instead more or less scat-tered hamlets of individual settlers whose small, irregular fields were fenced and hedged as they were cleared and, to use the old word, 'cured'. It is surely significant that it was in those parts where the enclosed field was historically earlier than the open field, which only appeared later during the second wave of village-founding, that the

Above: *The timelessness of Epping Forest.* Below: *a wood pile ready for burning into charcoal. The wood is arranged in careful formation so that it will burn evenly.*

A mound of earth is built around a great edifice of wood, the fire lit, and the charcoal-burners begin their work.

This picture, taken in the nineteenth century, shows a charcoal burner's wigwam in the Forest of Dean.

common field was first abandoned and all the farmland enclosed: such was the case in, for example, both Devonshire and Kent.

There were reasons of another kind why it was quite simply easier to abandon the common field in some places than in others: for example, in country which was short of pasture beyond the cultivated zone, the villagers depended on the stubble of the vast, unhedged cornfields to graze their cattle. Whereas in still-wooded country, where the farms were clearances in the forest, there was rough grazing for the cattle without this reliance on stubble fields; in such country the peasants were much less unwilling to see the land enclosed.

Now ditches were dug completely round each holder's land, and the spoil thrown up on the inside to form a bank. This long mound was then planted with hedging shrubs – hawthorn was the commonest one used, but sometimes some other plant would be chosen, or a mixture of hawthorn, blackthorn and maple. And since people were beginning to realize that the primeval forest would not last for ever and was, indeed, vanishing so fast that in some districts firing was already hard to come by, men of vision also planted young trees in these new banks – hazel, ash, maple, oak and elm. It was not intended that the trees be allowed to grow to their full stature, of course: they were to be coppice wood, to supply the farmer with poles, cord-wood for fuel and, in some cases, industrial raw material, for example oak-bark for the tanners. In short, hedgerow timber was a crop.

The first enclosed fields of this kind were, therefore, entire holdings and might be forty or fifty acres in extent. Apparently such fields were too big for the good management of the farm; for one thing they provided only inadequate shelter for cattle; so such holdings were divided up into smaller fields by more banks and hedges. Such was the process which first made rural England and the lowlands of Scotland look as so much of it still does.

But it was not, again, the only one: in other parts of the country a very different kind of enclosure was changing the look of the land. It will be remembered that, as a consequence of the shortage of labour and the steep rise in wages following the appallingly high mortality of the Black Death epidemic, landlords took to abandoning arable farming, getting rid of their few remaining tenants, razing villages and making vast sheep-runs which could be managed by a few hands. This produced an enormous increase in the sheep population. The large profits to be made by exporting wool – the origin, by the way, of our special interest in the Low Countries, our best customers for wool, which has had such a powerful influence on our foreign policy – soon led to the making of more and more such sheep-runs even after its social expediency had disappeared. This, of course, threw hundreds of poor peasants out of work at home, and created the problem of large-scale begging and vagabondage, which Elizabeth's governments had to deal with. Some modern research historians are of the opinion that the dispossession of peasants was not on such a scale, nor the suffering so bad as earlier social historians believed. But both certainly occurred on a considerable scale, or the first Poor Laws would not have been necessary.

Was it at this time, perhaps, that that doggerel verse was written which was so bitterly quoted during the eighteenth century, 'Parliamentary' enclosures?

> *The law condemns both man and woman*
> *Who steals a goose from off the common*
> *But lets the greater robber loose*
> *Who steals the common from the goose.*

The landlords who, from early in the sixteenth or late in the fifteenth century, took to evicting their tenants from their homes and turning them out of their livelihood to make sheep pastures, enclosed these pastures. Nor were they only sheep-runs which were depriving the poor of subsistence but putting big profits into landowners' pockets; for beef and hides were also very profitable cash crops as the towns grew; and the graziers were making fortunes.

Yet it is not possible to condemn totally these great enclosures as pernicious, cruel though they certainly were. They improved the quality of farming; they made experiment possible; they resulted in the accumulation of wealth for new investment; many Tudor enclosing landlords used their profits well: they built and furnished fine churches, built better, larger houses, planted miles of hedgerow timber in country which had been largely deforested, increased the numbers and improved the breeds of cattle and sheep. Complaints from the dispossessed peasantry were naturally long and loud, and not always unheard: there were occasions when the government forced enclosing landlords to restore the land to tillage, rebuild razed cottages and even whole villages, and give the people back their livelihood.

Still, in most cases, the change was permanent or at best postponed. Hundreds of villages disappeared, whole parishes were depopulated, and the ancient patchwork pattern of the open field was replaced in more

Oak trees in Richmond Park.

and more parts of Britain by enormous enclosed pastures. It should be noted that this change was not complete: the open field lasted over a vast area of England into the eighteenth century, and even – just – into the nineteenth.

The enormous enclosures, often exceeding 1,000 acres, which were the first consequence of this change-over from corn-growing to the growing of wool and meat, did not last long in that form. The proper management of sheep and cattle on intensive lines requires the control of their feeding, and for that purpose rather smaller fields were found to be better. So the first huge enclosures were divided by more banks and hedges here, as well as in the older enclosed counties, to form the very large permanent pasture fields characteristic of the midlands.

In many cases villagers had common rights which could not be ignored. (The device of using Acts of Parliament to get rid of them had not yet been used.) In such cases the enclosing landlord had to come to some agreement with the freeholders, either buying each freeholder's strips in the common field for cash or, where the freeholder refused to go elsewhere to earn his living, by giving him some small enclosed fields in exchange for his strips. That is the process which accounts for the existence of smaller hedged fields in the midlands amid the larger ones.

Dispossessed peasants were not the only people who disliked and feared the process of enclosure which transformed the old Britain into the new. For a hundred years, beginning with the reign of Henry VIII, governments, foreseeing a shortage of wheat and shrinking from the cost of helping the thousands of beggars who roamed the land and infested the towns, set their faces against the change. But their measures to check it were wholly ineffectual: the spirit of the age was against them.

By mid-eighteenth century there still remained a great deal of waste-land and even forest though the proportion of cultivated land to waste was now two thirds to one third. But inevitably we use the land and change it to our purpose; and this does not necessarily degrade the natural scene; it is perfectly possible to make all of it a work of beauty.

Enclosure from both the common field and the waste land continued. In England each case was covered by a Private Act of Parliament of which there were something like 2,000 between 1760 and 1820, bringing more and more country into hedged and banked fields and pastures. 'Parliamentary' enclosure was not the only kind. Rich land-owners were also enclosing wastes and commons illegally; and partly because the people were too poor and ignorant to offer any resistance to this private robbery of public property, partly because it was a good idea to have

An ash tree, showing very clearly the distinctive shape of its branches.

An ancient pasture on old Romney Marsh.

more and more land producing food, wool and hides, they usually got away with it. 'Property is Theft' said the French anarchist Proudhon, meaning property in resources which by natural law belong to all men in common. And certainly a great deal of landed property in Britain was theft. Sometimes opposition was strong enough to prevent enclosure, and ancient common was preserved; otherwise every square yard of England would have been included in some private estate, and such treasured commons as Epping Forest, now preserved for the people, would have been lost.

So the old patchwork pattern of common field strips, first laid down over the land by Saxon immigrants, disappeared, though not utterly until mid-nineteenth century, and all farmed England, and in due course the Welsh and Scottish lowlands, were covered with the banked and hedged fields which had made their first appearance in the twelfth century. Unable to compete against rich capitalist farmers, the tenants of great land-owners, or against land-owning farmers themselves, the small, free peasant farmers, and the class of yeomen, became fewer and fewer; and this brought about more change to the pattern of fields, pastures and orchards.

Looking at the picture more closely, the detail of the pattern was changing. Until the eighteenth century the method of sowing corn thick by broadcast scattering had not changed since, say, 7000 B.C. As a result of Jethro Tull's experiments and his text-book *Horse-hoeing Husbandry* (1733), wheat, barley and oats were drilled, which gave a new look to the cornfields. And the same great man's work led to another diversification of the pattern of agriculture: Tull taught farmers to grow turnips and sainfoin for winter feed, although they were very slow to learn. Fortunately, his principles were adopted by a great Norfolk land-owner, Lord Townsend, who thus became known as 'Turnip' Townsend.

Another great Norfolk land-owner who changed the face of his county and, by extension, of much more than Norfolk, by taking Tull seriously, and with some ideas of his own, was Thomas Coke of Holkham. He combined Tull's notions with the very old technique of 'marling' – that is, ploughing clay into sandy soil – and turned a waste of rabbit warrens into the most fertile cornfields and turnip fields in Europe, growing swedes as winter feed for cattle on a vast scale. The problem of keeping the herds and flocks alive throughout the winter, instead of slaughtering all but a few in late autumn as the prehistoric Windmill Hill people and all their successors in Britain had had to do, was solved. Coke also organized 'Holkham Gatherings' (1778–1821) for

A farmer and his man hoe mangels on his farm at Parracombe, Devon, in an area of England which has been consistently farmed for over a thousand years.

the exchange of new agricultural knowledge; they were attended by farmers and land-owners from all over Britain and in due course from all over the world – there were 7,000 guests at the 1821 gathering. The result of all this was that in England alone two million acres of wasteland were brought under cultivation.

Since the creatures living on the face of England are a part of the scene, and the greatest change in that scene in the nineteenth century was the proliferation of man, we must consider what changes occurred in the aspect of the country's livestock, changes analogous to those which had from time to time taken place in the British face and other physical attributes: in any city street, at any country fair or in any market place, all the faces of the past could still be seen: small, lively dark people whose ancestors were here before the Aryan invasions; red-heads of Celtic stock; dark-haired round-heads from the Mediterranean basin; and the big, blue-eyed, fair- or brown-haired people of Germanic derivation.

Now came a great change in the aspect of their animals.

The pioneer of this change was a man born at Dishley near Loughborough, Robert Bakewell (1725–95), who, anticipating modern genetical science, realized that the shape of an animal and all its attrib-

The Earl of Leicester, one of the famous gentlemen sheep farmers, who set out to improve breeding.

utes could be changed by selective breeding. The results of cross-breeding had long been realized; Bakewell saw that it would be possible to breed, by careful selection of parent animals over several generations, for pre-determined attributes. Because England and Wales had become the greatest wool-producing countries in Europe, their sheep had come to be regarded as wool-producing animals, with their mutton as a mere by-product. Bakewell set out to breed sheep which would supply as much good meat as possible and fine fleece as well. At a time when out-breeding was regarded as essential to the health of flocks, Bakewell boldly resorted to in-breeding; he was, in fact, the pioneer of what is now called 'line-breeding'. He succeeded in 'making' a sheep with small bones, a massive barrel-shaped body carrying a maximum of good mutton and a good fleece: this animal, the Leicester breed, became world-famous. From this time forward, sheep were no longer scraggy, rangy animals like woolly goats, but tubby as we know them now.

Bakewell's successes with cattle and with cart horses were not as striking as his success with sheep; yet he did alter the look of them.

It is important to remember that farm animals in Britain did not always look as they do now: one of the striking things in a foreign landscape when one is travelling, is that the animals in the fields look different. I do not mean only in very remote countries. I am not talking of such obviously different animals as Indian humped cattle and water-buffaloes, or the goat-like sheep of the eastern Mediterranean; even just across the Channel this different look is there for those who have eyes to see. The cattle of pre-Bakewell England were as different from our cattle, as the cattle of Greece or southern Italy are today. There is, in short, nothing 'immemorial' in the face of Britain: the patterns made by foliage, by the shapes and habits of trees and lesser plants and the works of man, are always new. 'Our' Britain is almost nowhere 'old'; it never was.

Another remarkable man whose influence at this time hastened the changes in Britain's face was Arthur Young, born in London of a Suffolk father and a Jewish mother, and educated in agricultural Suffolk. He took a small farm to put some ideas about farming into practice, and failed with it; and as a practical farmer he failed repeatedly. He toured the south of England and wrote a book about its farming; did the same thing in the north; then in Ireland where the oppression of the Catholic peasantry by the Protestant ascendancy horrified him; then France and Italy – looking, asking, listening, noting and writing. His ability, common sense and understanding of the farmer's practical problems won him such a following that he changed the face of farming, not only in Britain but in France. So that it scarcely mattered that his ideals, his passion for good farming and an advanced, capitalist rural economy were never understood by the practical men, since they nevertheless put his ideas into practice.

Young hated the suffering of the peasantry entailed in the policy of enclosure, but saw clearly that, economically, enclosures were right. He foresaw the benefits of enormously increased production from the land which would follow the completion of enclosures of the common fields and the taking of the remaining waste into cultivation; he also saw with painful clarity that those benefits would go into the pockets of the big farmers and the rich land-owners, while the common people went short as usual. But his aim was to increase the gross national product, for in the long run everyone must be better off because of that; in achieving that aim, by his writings, he promoted more great changes in the physiognomy of the land.

1 *The Long-Horned or*
Lancaster Breed

2 *The Improved*
Holstein or Dutch Breed

3 *The Holstein or*
Dutch Breed

4 *Wild Cattle*

Thomas Bewick, the famous engraver, first published his History of Quadrupeds *in 1790. It featured many breeds of cattle and oxen including the so-called 'improved' breeds.*

5   *Wild Cattle*

6   *The Improved
Holstein or Dutch Breed*

7   *The Lancashire Ox*

8   *The Holstein or
Dutch Breed*

The Fenlands bordering the Bedford river, Cambridgeshire.

At several points in this history we have paid attention to the subject of draining the morasses of the east midlands. Saxons, Danes and Normans all had a hand in turning some fen country into farmland; much of their work was undone by the forced neglect following the Black Death. Just before the time of the Stuarts, Dutch capitalists were beginning to invest money in the Lincolnshire and Cambridgeshire fens, and Dutch engineers to undertake drainage schemes. Then, in Stuart times, the pace of this movement accelerated, Dutch capital and skill were invested in the fens on a large scale, and the Dutchmen had to meet the fierce opposition of the people of the fens whose way of life and livelihood depended on the watery conditions. That opposition sometimes flared into violence. But the fen-men's resistance to change was ineffectual: the Dutchmen had royal licences; the Court had a financial interest in the success of the big drainage schemes, and the works and foreign workers were protected by both law and detachments of soldiers.

Early in the seventeenth century the Great Fens, from Lincolnshire to south Cambridgeshire, were all wild country – shallow meres and pools, bogs and morasses, with some islands of solid land populated by small communities of wild-fowlers, eel-catchers, fishermen and people who got their living by cutting and selling osier and reed. The great Dutch engineer, Cornelius Vermuyden, employing Dutch workmen, transformed 400,000 acres of this waste into rich, fertile land. This was one of the greatest changes wrought in the land's face by one, deliberate, planned operation.

Drainage of another kind also made a contribution to change: the old way to get rid of surface water was to plough the fields into high ridges separated by furrows which carried off the water. With that water went, in solution, the nutrient salts required by the plants; thus fertility was continuously lost and, incidentally, the value of manuring largely wasted. New methods entailed digging very deep trenches which were then covered in again; and, later, the planting of shallow tile-drains (half-pipes) filled with stones at intervals below the surface of the fields, these drains having outfalls into the ditches. This meant that water carrying nutrients in solution was fed to the roots of the plants and some of it trapped as soil-water, before the surplus was drained off. It also meant that some of the wrinkles were smoothed out of Britain's skin.

7   Homes and Gardens

The extensive new building and rebuilding which the profits of the wool trade and rising industries made possible in Tudor times did much to change the look of both town and country.

Early in this epoch a new feature was added to the countryside: the gentleman's house, as distinct from the lord's castle. Henry VII tamed the warrior aristocracy which had for centuries disturbed the peace of England with inter-baronial warfare; and there was no danger of invasion from abroad. Once the Wars of the Roses were over, the castle became pointless.

Typical of the great new houses and of the way in which they came to be built was Compton Wynyates in Warwickshire. First, as a consequence of a licensed enclosure of 2,000 acres by Sir William Compton in 1510, the village of Compton Superior was emptied of its inhabitants, who were simply turned out of doors, and razed. Two years later Sir William set about making himself a park and building his grand house. His building materials came from the ruins of another village, Fullbrook, which had been occasioned when the Duke of Bedford – that Regent of France defeated by Joan of Arc – had formed one of the earliest great enclosures in the midlands nearly a century earlier.

Great country houses rose all over England, founded on the misery of a generation. At least they were beautiful. The earliest were hall-houses in the medieval style, with a muddle of wings and outbuildings so that they had no particular shape inside or out, for the great halls were ceiled or divided into two floors and several rooms. Later in the sixteenth century came properly designed Renaissance houses built under Continental influence but in a style which became more and more specifically native. These were the great Elizabethan houses, and some of them were enormous palaces, monuments to the vulgar ostentation of a newly rich class spending the loot of the dissolution of the monasteries and the profits from wool. Holdenby, for example, was nearly twice the size of Blenheim, the palace which the nation was to build for the Duke of Marlborough two centuries later. Burghley, Montacute, Longleat, Kirby Hall, Knole, Hardwicke Hall ('more glass than wall') and Audley End are surviving, or partially surviving, examples of these great private palaces so much grander than England's or Scotland's royal palaces. To this period belongs James IV of Scotland's Great Hall, Edinburgh, and his Renaissance palace at Stirling.

As well as these grandiose piles of brick and stone bearing heavily on Britain's face, there was a very much greater number of smaller houses going up. The few hundreds of medieval hall-houses gave way to thousands of much more comfortable houses with a number of rooms. Where it was available, they were built of local freestone. Brick was used in the brick-earth districts and, because the soil there is best for fruit-trees, orchards of apple, pear and cherry were being planted. Elsewhere, there was a half-timbered style with beam and plaster.

The very beautiful Elizabethan manor house, Compton Wynyates in Warwickshire.

Longleat.

Villages throughout those parts of Britain where freestone was abundant were rebuilt as small towns entirely of stone: the sheep, with its golden fleece, did for vast areas of England what Augustus did for Rome – found it timber and left it stone. In the villages where there was no local stone, brick or half timbering was used. Even small houses acquired a second floor and, with the fall in glass prices following technological advances in the glass industry, properly glazed windows. Not all the money for this investment in building came from wool. Farming boomed as the urban markets for wheat and meat grew. Prices for farm products kept rising, while costs remained stable. Something had to be done with the surplus. And because communications were still bad, so that the movement of heavy or bulky materials from one part of Britain to another was costly and very laborious, each community delved into the ground under its feet for its building material, so that vernacular architecture became a sort of man-made expression of the land's geology.

Above: *Hardwicke Hall, Derbyshire, from the west.* Below: *Montacute House, in Somerset, from the north-east.*

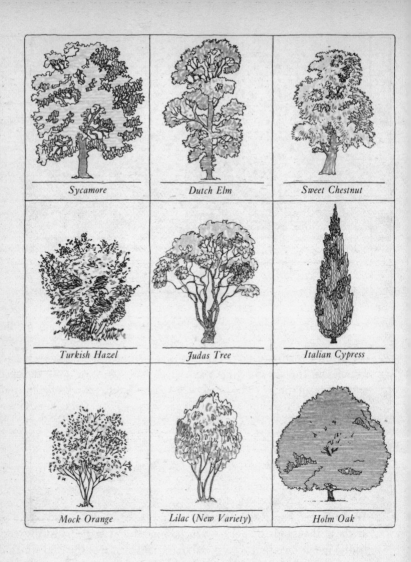

Sycamore	Dutch Elm	Sweet Chestnut
Turkish Hazel	Judas Tree	Italian Cypress
Mock Orange	Lilac (New Variety)	Holm Oak

Above and opposite above: *Trees introduced into eighteenth-century English country gardens.*

Walnut   Acacia

A number of tree species were now introduced into Britain for the first time, kinds of trees which seem to us immemorial in the rural scene, but which are not. Among the most important were sycamore, Dutch elm and the sweet chestnut which had almost or quite vanished since Roman times. The pine was reintroduced into England from Scotland, the larch into Scotland from Norway. The Turkish hazel was planted in nut orchards in Kent and Sussex and the Judas Tree, the Italian Cypress, the Mock Orange and the lilac appeared for the first time in the great gardens of the rural and urban palaces. Holm-oak, walnut and the tree we call acacia (it is really a *Robinia*) began to appear in ornamental plantings of trees.

We have seen how the shape of our fields came about. We can now look at those thousands of houses which, adored and copied (usually very badly) in our own time, composed that countenance of the land which is expressed in the cliché Olde Englande. The specimen case we will look at is that of Barton's End in Kent.

Richard Barton was a wealthy Kentish squire who, being a Protestant in the reign of Mary Tudor, was obliged to remain quiet on his estate rather than take his place in the running of the country's business, for fear of drawing too much attention to himself. He thus spent his time and energies improving his land and house: both he and his wife, and also their children, were readers, and his house had a small collection of books on the latest advances in good husbandry. He had managed to enclose his land without rousing the hostility of the local peasants and he had invested largely in sheep, so that he was in on the ground floor of the wool boom. When his younger son John returned home, at the age of eighteen (1554), after spending eight years on his uncle's estate near Guildford in Surrey, Barton decided that, rather than upset the peasants by enclosing more common land, it would be wise, in his circumstances, to create a farmstead for the young man by clearing wasteland and forest, the sort of country his own estate was surrounded by and included.

This labour of clearance, and the building of a suitable house, would require capital. Fortunately, there was money in hand: in the years 1554 and 1555 the price of wool in the Flemish markets remained high, and the Barton wool-clip was a very good one. Sold in Rye to the wool exporters, these two wool-clips fetched a lot of money. Moreover, Barton had betrothed his son John to the sixteen-year-old daughter of a rich neighbour, and Mary Halstead brought with her the very satisfactory jointure of £100 – something like £3,000 of our money.

A suitable site in newly cleared wasteland and forest was chosen – dry, but near a source of water. In fact, three sites were chosen before the water-diviner decided on one where a well could be sunk and yet the land was firm and well-drained. The well was dug and proved before anything else was done, for the Bartons had experience of the troubles of houses which had been built without proper attention being paid to a convenient supply of good water.

The plan of the house was roughly sketched on paper, and then marked out on the ground with pegs and strings. It was designed to lie north-east to south-west, so that the morning sun would light the bedrooms and get the sleepers up and about, while the evening sun would light the kitchen and parlour enabling work and reading to be continued late. The house was to be about sixty feet long and thirty feet wide. The ground floor was to have a big central kitchen, separated from the parlour by the brickwork chimney-breast and fireplaces, a dairy and a storeroom. The bricks probably came from the east Kent brickfields. The upper floor had a big 'landing' for the staircase, a master-bedroom, a sons' bedroom, a daughters' bedroom, a maid-servant's room, a man-servant's room and a guest room. The bedrooms were warmed by the chimney-breast which passed through them. Modernized, such houses still make some of the most pleasant homes in England.

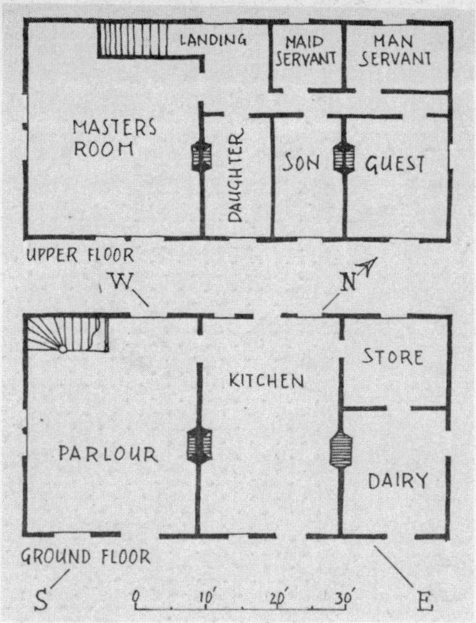
LANDING
MAID SERVANT
MAN SERVANT
MASTERS ROOM
DAUGHTER
SON
GUEST
UPPER FLOOR
W
N
STORE
KITCHEN
PARLOUR
DAIRY
GROUND FLOOR
S
0
10'
20'
30'
E

A ground- and first-floor plan of Barton's End, in Kent.

A cut-away diagram showing the method of building a half timbered and wattle and daub house.

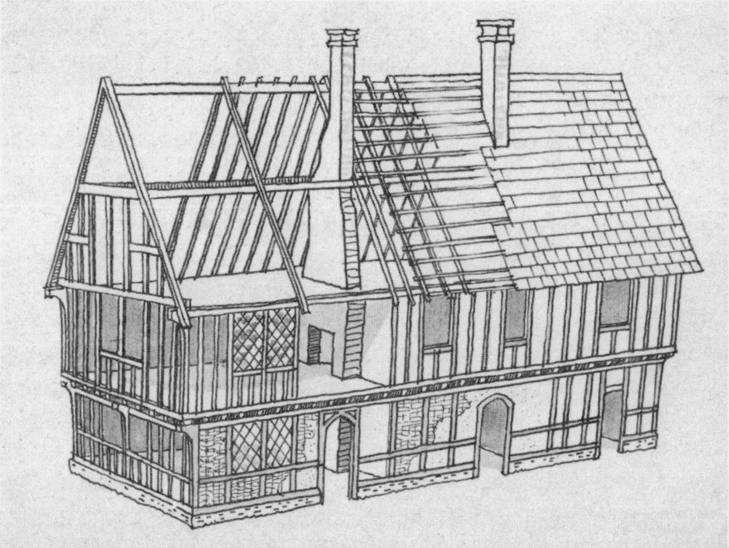

As this was not one of the freestone or brick-earth regions, the principal material required was timber. The estate sawyers were set to work on the oaks which had been felled in making the clearing, to saw the quantity of beams and planks required, that quantity being calculated from the ground plan; there were no architects for such houses – the people were their own architects or they left the details of design to the chief carpenter. The sawing took up the whole winter of 1554–5 and the material was ready by the spring. But because mature timber was better for the principal beams of the house, Barton had one of his wagons, which had gone to Rye with a load of wool, make the return journey with a load of old ships' timbers from the shipyards of that port.

The common practice in the building of half-timbered houses as simple as this one was to put the framework of the walls together on the ground, the joints being morticed and dowelled, for a minimum of iron was used. The wall was then heaved upright by means of ropes, half the parish lending a hand, and braced in the vertical plane while the other wall frames were pulled upright and dowelled together. Those spaces in the framework not intended for windows or doors were filled with locally-made wattle and daub made from any convenient source of clay. This rough work was afterwards plastered more or less neatly. In the 1950s I had to do a small repair to the daub-and-wattle wall of a house built a few years before Barton's End, and when the wattle was exposed it was found to be as good as the day it was put in: in that case it appeared to be made of willow, but other flexible woods were also used.

By August 1555 the roof ridge of Barton's End was in place and its placing was duly celebrated, a flag being flown to announce this progress to the parish so that any neighbours who wanted to do so could call and see the work and congratulate the family. Then the windows were put in, the doors hung and the flue tried to make sure that it did not smoke backwards into the kitchen and parlour, and the house sealed to dry until the spring, under its thatch roof. John Barton and Mary Halstead were married in March 1556 and began life in their new house.

Thousands of houses of this kind, built not only in beam and plaster but in brick and stone, sprang up all over the land in the sixteenth century, in both town and country, sketching that aspect of England which still attracts several million tourists every summer.

While such simple and comfortable houses were contributing a feature to Britain's face which was to be a permanent element of the aspect of man-made Britain, building of a nobler sort than gentlemen's manors,

The Chapel, New College, Oxford. A beautiful example of Perpendicular Gothic.

noblemen's palaces or yeomen's houses (the labourer's cottage was still a mud hovel) was contributing something else.

English Gothic was never as grand, never as awe-inspiring in sheer bulk, as French Gothic. Perhaps its relative modesty in dimension and the perfection of its proportions are expressions of the national moderation. At all events, Gothic developed forms and details of beauty in England never seen anywhere else. It is almost impossible to stand back and take in at one glance the magnificence of the grandest examples of French or German Gothic; but at, say, Wells or Lichfield, one can see the whole building and see that it is a perfect work of art. That is not the only difference: for there were English stone-carvers who, for example, introduced a just measure of stylization into foliage carving; excelled in the decoration of façades with figures; and there were English masons who expressed a sense of proportion as exquisite as the Italian, in their arcading.

But sixteenth-century 'Perpendicular' Gothic ecclesiastical architecture was a continuation of the fourteenth-century work. What the Tudor phase of Gothic added to England was a secular modification best seen in the Oxford colleges founded and built between 1500 and 1550. Not that college architecture would then have been called 'secular', of course, but it is only in such building that Gothic was used for anything but churches in Britain until the nineteenth century; we never built anything like the Cloth Hall at Ypres, the Town Hall at Bruges or the magnificent Town Hall of Brussels. But that college Gothic of the Tudors was to be taken up again and brilliantly repeated in the eighteenth century.

King Henry VII and his successor, Henry VIII, made a small beginning to the introduction in England, from Italy, of the new 'classical' architecture of the Renaissance, based, in its relative simplicity and purity of line, on the ancient Greek and the best Roman; for both of them employed an Italian architect, Torrigiano, a friend of Benvenuto Cellini, on building works. (Cellini had designed Henry VII's tomb.) But the real pioneers of the new style in England were Inigo Jones and Christopher Wren. Jones (1573–1652) studied architecture and, by the way, theatrical designing, in Italy. Two good examples of his work are the Banqueting Hall in Whitehall Palace and the Queen's House at Greenwich (now part of the Maritime Museum). Inigo Jones did his best work between about 1615 and 1635. Christopher Wren (1632–1723) never managed a journey to Italy, but he did study the new architecture in France where it had become fashionable earlier. His great monument is, of course, London's St Paul's Cathedral. There, his plan for the rebuilding of London, after the Great Fire had destroyed so much of the old city, is kept and nothing could be more Italianate than that plan.

In Scotland, Sir William Bruce rebuilt the main front of the Palace of Holyroodhouse in the new style: this was done in the reign of Charles II but the king's grandfather, James VI and I, had started the reshaping of the palace before his return visit in 1617; '. . . in respect he would be convoyit and conducted be certain nobles of Ingland he wald let them know that this countrie was nothing inferior to theirs in anie respect'. James had wanted to employ Inigo Jones on part of the work but was dissuaded by the Scottish bishops, afraid that Jones's ideas of decoration would offend the Presbyterians. When it came to Charles's turn, he personally instructed Sir William Bruce, who was '. . . to design and order the building . . . in pillar work to conform to and with the Dorick and Ionic orders and finish the ends above the platform of the front order, agreeing with the Corinthian style'.

Until well into the eighteenth century agriculture in Scotland, and therefore the look of the land, remained medieval, with the result, by the way, that the misery of the peasantry was extreme, and years of famine with great loss of life, from starvation, frequent (1709, 1740, 1760). The Scots were at first much slower than the English to adopt the new ways of farming and the new crops: even turnip, which in England was saving the cattle even during the hardest winters, was regarded as a rich land-owner's fad. When in the second half of the eighteenth century Scottish land-owners began afforestation, their saplings were uprooted by the indignant peasantry; but that story belongs to the next chapter.

While farmers and improving landlords were completing the job of giving agricultural Britain – which by the end of the nineteenth century meant nearly all rural England, lowland Wales and Scotland, with less and less wilderness remaining – that aspect which is what we mean when we think of 'the country', change of an entirely new kind was being wrought by a very different kind of men: those remarkable artists who turned hundreds of gentlemen's parks into landscape pictures.

There are hundreds of 'views' embracing thousands of acres each, which those who know nothing of the history of Britain's face point out to each other, exclaim over, admire, photograph and describe as aspects of the country's natural beauty, but which are the antithesis of works of nature – that is, they are works of art.

I call the English landscaping movement entirely new for two

Christopher Wren's plan of the City of London after the Great Fire of 1666.

William Kent by B. Dandridge.

reasons: Italian and French landscape gardening, deriving from the Roman which derived from the Near Eastern, were aspects of architecture and were wholly formal; in short, the English landscaping art owed nothing to European gardening though it owed much to European painting. It is true that something very like it has a long and fascinating history in ancient China, and in Japan; and Continental critics have suggested a connection.

There was no such connection; a careful examination of the chronology of the influence on English style of European travellers in China makes that very clear. In other words, a similarity in the approach to nature of the ancient Chinese gentry and of the eighteenth-century English gentry had a similar outcome, but that is all.

The transformation of some hundreds of thousands of acres of England and Wales began when such travelled and cultivated noblemen as Lord Burlington brought back to England a taste for Italian and French landscape painting, and Italian neo-Hellenic architecture. They communicated this taste to the garden artists and architects whom they 'patronized' and sometimes sent abroad to study the subjects on the spot.

The pioneer of the idea of changing whole real landscapes into pictures (instead of painting landscapes on canvas), was Burlington's protégé, William Kent (1685–1748). For although there were some considerable English landscape gardeners before him, their work was in the French or Dutch 'architectural' taste. Kent, some of whose work still survives at Rousham and at Stowe, had as his assistant at Stowe the young head-gardener, formerly a kitchen-gardener and before that a gardener's boy, Launcelot ('Capability') Brown.

Brown (1716–83) who, despite his parents' relative poverty, had had a sound basic education, learned so fast that it was he who completed the work which Kent began at Stowe; and who did it, moreover, in terms which he had already worked out for himself, and which were not merely those of his master. Thus, although he was not the first, he was the greatest exponent of this new English art. Kent, Brown, his successor Repton, and their lesser imitators, created irregular, romantic landscapes, bringing hills, trees and buildings into a harmony of relations which was very little 'natural' and wholly 'picturesque'. But whereas Kent, more nearly under the influence of Continental painting (he had studied in Rome), made much use of temples, semi-formal cascades and many statues, Brown excelled in using only earth, trees and water – hence the fact that much of his work can be taken for nature's, although he himself never had any doubt that he excelled her, and once, beholding one of his picturesque water-and-landscapes, exclaimed that the Thames would never forgive him. Examples of Brown's work can still be seen at Benham, Speen in Berkshire, at Stowe in Buckinghamshire, at Chatsworth in Derbyshire, at Milton Abbas in Dorset, at Longleat on the Wiltshire–Somerset border, at Harewood House, Yorkshire, and in many other places.

This great artist manipulated square miles of his country at a time, created grand lakes, changed the courses of rivers and the profiles of hills, and planted hundreds of thousands of trees (the number probably amounts to millions), in creating his magnificent landscape pictures. He was accused of being a destroyer of trees, but for every one he felled, he planted many. Realizing that park, garden and house should be a unity, he taught himself architecture so that he could build houses as well, usually in the fashionable 'Palladian' style introduced from Italy by Burlington, but sometimes in a revival of the Tudor Gothic style.

On at least two occasions he razed whole villages and rebuilt them elsewhere as model villages; this was not, of course, for the betterment of the villagers who were thus rehoused, but to remove an incongruity

Above:
'Capability' Brown's plan for the gardens at Sherborne Castle.

Left: *'Capability' Brown, painted by N. Dance.*

131

from the view. As Brown worked extremely hard all his life on hundreds of estates, becoming, in the process, the friend of England's leading men and notably of the king, George III, himself, and affectionately known as 'Capability' Brown, and as he had scores of imitators, including his own assistants, his influence on the look of England was probably greater than that of any other man in all her history.

But another ran him very close: his artistic successor Humphry Repton (1752–1818), son of an excise officer, educated in Holland at the house of a great merchant, musician and amateur painter of talent. He began his working life in business, became a country gentleman on a small estate when his parents died leaving him money, and was, for a while, personal assistant to the Secretary for Ireland. Long interested in gardening, in forestry and in architecture, he also wrote sketches and art criticisms for a periodical, and a play called *Odd Whims* which was staged in Norwich. When his way of life and his large family ran him perilously close to bankruptcy, he took up landscape gardening as a means of earning a living, and was an almost immediate success. Recognizing Brown as his master, he nevertheless had his own personal, more flexible and more 'natural' style. Like Brown he manipulated very large tracts of country, made lakes, planted trees on a lavish scale and transformed hundreds of estates into pictures. Not only did he become an architect himself, but two of his sons were architects and for some time he was in working partnership with Nash.

These and many lesser professional landscape gardeners were not the only people helping at this time to turn England into a landscape painter's dream. Hundreds of land-owners were practitioners of this new art, some of them had talent and one or two – for example, Richard Payne Knight, and Henry Hoare who created the masterpiece of Stourhead – had something like genius. Sir Gilbert Heathcote of Normanton demolished a medieval village and church to get his 'prospect' right, rebuilding both elsewhere; Wimpole in Cambridgeshire, Burton Constable in Yorkshire, Milton Abbas, Budby near Thoresby Park were other villages which were destroyed and rebuilt for the same reasons. Brown was almost certainly the architect of Milton Abbas, although the credit is often given to his bitter enemy Sir William Chambers, and to both of them we owe the landscaping of Kew Gardens. In the same way, some of the work attributed to Nash was really the work of Repton, to whom we owe the handsomest of the London squares gardens, and the idea of making Regent's Park a great landscape garden surrounded by 'Palladian' terraces.

The gardens at Stourhead.

All over Britain country houses in the new Grecian or Italianate styles either replaced the older ones, or were built for the first time, often in Brown or Repton parks.

Gentlemen of means, acting belatedly on John Evelyn's plea in *Sylva* for new afforestation to make good the forest depredations of iron-workers and ship-builders, planted trees by the hundred thousand. Species of trees never seen before in Britain began to diversify the scene early in the nineteenth century – many new firs, spruces and pines from America and the east of Europe brought a touch of evergreen into the winter scene. Many new shrubs, including new kinds of roses, appeared in thousands of great gardens. Orchards of improved apples and pears, cherries and plums from France and the Low Countries spread wider in the brick-earth counties, and in Kent, Sussex and Herefordshire the pretty pattern of hop-gardens grew more extensive as the consumption of beer rose with urban populations.

Perhaps it was in Scotland that the face of Britain changed most dramatically in this epoch. Here resistance to change was much greater than in England and Wales. Agricultural 'improvers' were hampered, in the application of new techniques, by differences in soils and climate, by archaic laws, customs and practices, by superstition and

Milton Abbas, Dorset. The church and cottages in 'Capability' Brown's ideal village.

poverty. The Scottish farmers hated trees, believing that they exhausted the land; and were as destructive of the 'improvers'' new plantations as goats are in the Middle East. But by 1750 change was beginning to be accepted. Scientific 'improvers' like Maxwell of Arkland, with his Society of Improvers of Knowledge and Agriculture, James and Andrew Meikle, inventors of the threshing-mill, the Duchess of Gordon, the Countess of Haddington, 'Potato' Wilkie of Ratho, Lord Kaines of Blair Drummond – drainer of the Kincardine marshes and author, in his eighties, of *The Gentleman Farmer* – both showed and led the way. The Turnpike Acts at last gave Scotland roads, and the 'Montgomery Act' enabled 'improving' landlords to settle a proportion of the expense of improvement on their successors; both facilitated change. In the Highlands, tenants were transported and sheep imported; it was a hideous injustice, inflicting atrocious misery on tens of thousands of people; but it increased the gross national product tenfold.

So, on Scotland's face, heather and gorse and marshland gave way to barley, wheat and oats, to forests and enormous pastures; villages grew into towns with the growth of trade. Where it was tameable, the land was tamed – to such effect that Brown's *History of Glasgow* records (1797) that '. . . a native who had left this country in 1760 on his return at this date would find himself only to be directed by the geography of the surrounding mountains'. .

New machines became a feature of the rural scene – drills, reaping, mowing and winnowing machines, threshing machinery, a horse-powered tedder for tossing hay, and all-iron ploughs and harrows to replace the older wooden tools.

8 Scars, Lines and Wrinkles

The story of the scarring, lining and wrinkling of Britain's face, of the premature ageing and disfigurement of great areas of land between the sixteenth and twentieth centuries, is incomprehensible without at least a brief glance at the subject of population. Fewer people could not have wrought such spectacular change, put such terrible scars and lines of labour on the land's face, scars and lines and wrinkles which, although far from pretty, are the marks of a people's life and of the character which they have imparted to their country.

There is another way of looking at it: we have noted that in the sixteenth century observant foreigners found the land remarkably empty; for so few people, it would not have been necessary to make such changes. Is industrialization the product of population increase, or population increase of industrialization? Each is the product of the other, they are mutually generating. And the process of population growth and the changes in the physiognomy of England are inextricable.

At some time in the sixteenth century the population recovered to the level it had reached just before the Black Death. It overtook that high point and during the next two centuries increased steadily but without any 'explosion'. By the end of the eighteenth century the population stood at about nine million. Then, with apparent suddenness, the rate of increase became 'explosive'. As I say, why it did so does not concern us here, and in any case social historians have yet to agree among themselves what the reasons were. Let a small list of figures speak for themselves:

1801:	8,893,000
1821:	12,000,000
1831:	15,914,000
1861:	20,066,000
1881:	25,974,000
1911:	36,070,000

From 1400 to 1800, four *centuries*, the population increased by six million; from 1800 to 1840, four *decades*, it increased by seven million; the rate of growth increased more than tenfold.

So that one might say that by far the greatest change on the face of Britain during the eighteenth and nineteenth centuries was the proliferation of one of the native species of large mammals, man; incidentally, at the expense of the others, although it is true that two of the three other large species, wolf and boar, were probably extinct at the end of the seventeenth century, leaving only the deer in the remainder of the forests and in gentlemen's parks.

The growth of industry, despite frequent checks, setbacks and long pauses, was a continuous process from the time of such flint-tool factories as Grimes Grave until today: there was no revolution; there was evolution; with feature after feature added, altering the shape and scarring it here and there, as our power to delve increased.

But it is virtually impossible to describe a continuous process in history: readers who are familiar with calculus will know what I mean when I say that we have no notation for describing, much less analysing, the infinitely small changes which add up to continuous change. One could perhaps draw a curve on squared paper to show the quantitative rise and increasing rate of rise of, say, the iron industry in Britain from 500 B.C. to A.D. 1973; what one could not do is to describe every tiny element composing that curve.

But it is true that at certain times there were great spurts forward in technology and in capital investment which made relatively large changes in a relatively short time: it is for this reason that historians have written of revolution in this context; there was such a spurt in the fourteenth century) there were probably earlier ones; one could write of the introduction of the wheeled plough as an industrial revolution); there was a tremendous jump in the late eighteenth and early nineteenth centuries; we are at this moment in the course of another; the one we are concerned with at this point in the story of the making of Britain's face is the technological spurt of the sixteenth and seventeenth centuries. And we are so concerned with it because, despite the existence of industries since prehistoric times, this was the first to make deep lines and wrinkles on Britain's face.

But one must not exaggerate: an observant centenarian still vigorous enough to walk over Britain in, say, 1680, and who had walked it as a boy of ten in 1590, would have seen great changes at certain points of his journey, but would have concluded, with the complacency of the old,

Fleet Street and Ludgate Hill leading up to St Paul's. Nineteenth-century view of the bustling, jostling, overcrowded streets of the city of London.

that Britain was Britain still – that is, the land he was born into. Thus, although this certainly was a period of rapidly expanding trade, with wool exports and later cloth exports as its mainstay; and although, in this period, British merchant shipping overhauled both the merchant shipping of the Hanseatic league and that of Venice – facts which imply changes on the face of Britain – industry still marked the land's face only lightly with new lines and wrinkles. For the workshops turning out cloth were private houses, hardly yet factories. And at the beginning of this period the medieval trading regulations were a serious check to growth: in the chartered towns no man could trade unless and until he was admitted to a guild as a master of his trade, and as the guilds restricted membership to protect their 'establishment', such boroughs were slow to grow. Early in the sixteenth century there were not more than a dozen towns with populations in excess of 10,000 people.

On the other hand, new towns, where trading was free, now began to grow fast, so that by the end of the sixteenth century they were providing employment in industry and trade for that part of the rural population which had been made redundant on the land because of the replacement of arable farming by sheep runs and graziers' pastures.

In England, the dissolution of the monasteries created, by the distribution of the monastic wealth to laymen, a new plutocracy more interested in making money than in accumulating land and tenants, provided the country with a class of capitalists looking for good investments and thus boosted industry and commerce – we are coming to that presently. This generated wealth for the building of more town houses and many more gentlemen's country houses. Tudor architecture in very elaborate 'black-and-white' half-timbering added to the face of England features like Lavenham's lovely Guild House in Suffolk, Trade Guild headquarters of the wool merchants; private houses like Handforth Hall, built by the Brereton family about 1562, Huddington Court in Worcestershire, Moreton Old Hall near Congleton in Cheshire. And there were also high streets like Shrewsbury's in the same style. It was now that England acquired that countenance which, in tourist eyes, is 'typically English'.

Growth of the ports was promoted by the Elizabethan boom in both legitimate sea-borne trade – in off-shore fishing, in naval building – and in the licensed piracy called privateering. These, in their turn, stimulated a boom in ship-building which again meant changes in the look of the coastal regions. House-building and ship-building demanded more and more timber, but as we shall see this was not the chief cause of

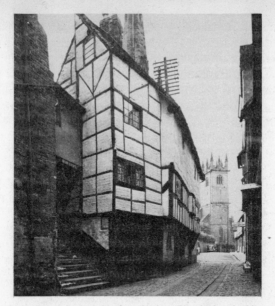

Shrewsbury High Street with its black and white Elizabethan buildings.

Lavenham Guildhall, Suffolk.

the worrying rise in timber prices and the serious shortage of wood which began to make itself felt.

Now there were big industrial developments, big enough to add, as I said above, lines and wrinkles of their own to the land's ageing face.

A first attempt to establish a paper-mill in Britain – our paper had until then all been imported – was made in 1500. It failed, but before the end of the century paper-mills driven by water power were established on a number of our rivers. Gun-powder mills, cannon foundries, works for making saltpetre and the first sugar-refineries were all added to the scene in the sixteenth century. Prospectors for minerals found zinc ore in Somerset which meant the founding of a new mining industry; at the same time, the mining of copper ore on a much larger scale than ever before was undertaken in the west country. These two mining industries not only added new scars to the face of Britain, but new wrinkles too since they promoted the building of foundries for the smelting of copper and zinc, and factories where copper plate, ingots and brass could be processed.

Around Whitby in Yorkshire the production of alum from alum stone was already an ancient industry: there is a local legend that the secret of this process had belonged to the Vatican and that the Chaloner family came under a papal curse for acquiring it by some more or less discreditable means. Now this industry developed, great wooden sheds were built for carrying on the work, housing furnaces, cisterns, huge metal pans for boiling the ingredients, and for stacking the considerable quantities of coal which was at last being used as fuel. This alum industry was one of those which called for the investment of large sums and the employment of many workers. George Lowe, one of the leading men in the business in 1619 wrote of it:

. . . a distracted worke in severall places and of sundry partes not possible to be performed by anie one man nor by a fewe. But by a multitude of the baser sort, of whom the most part are idle, careless and false in their labour.[1]

The long battle of recriminations between capital and labour had begun.

Industry in other fields grew out of the farmhouse and cottage, into the factory, starting a new kind of work on the land's face. John Browne, cannon-founder to Charles I and later Parliamentary gun-maker during the Civil War, employed 200 workers at his gun factory at Brenchley in Kent. At Dartford there was a paper-mill run by a German immigrant

[1] Lansdowne MSS. quoted by J. U. Nef in *Essays in Economic History*, ed. E. M. Carus-Wilson. London, 1961.

technician where, according to one account, no less than 600 men were employed. Such big industrial plants had to be on rivers, of course, since their machinery was driven by water-wheels. The kind of investment involved can be judged from the figure of £1,400 (say £30–40,000 in today's terms) paid for converting the water-wheel machinery at Dartford from its original job of blowing a blast-furnace (see below) to that of working the paper-making presses.

The production of saltpetre, sugar and brass, all new industries, was carried on in smaller establishments than those needed for alum or paper, and most of the cannon-foundries were not large. But, after wool and cloth, guns soon became England's first great export line, and English guns were in great demand in the Continental countries because of their quality and their cheapness.

More considerable changes in the look of Britain were brought about by another kind of industrial development, the introduction from the Continent of new techniques which speeded the growth and changed the nature of some older industries.

Among the ugliest man-made scars on Britain's face are those of coal-mining: whole districts have been devastated by it in the course of getting the wealth out of the ground. But for a reason which will be presently clear I think it better to deal with the subject of coal a little later – when we have used up all the wood. Here all I need to say is that there were now great technological advances in coal-mining which made possible the development of other industries by increasing the supplies of coal.

There were still further advances now in the mining of metal ores: what formerly had been not much more than a scratching of the surface became very deep digging on an extensive scale, with shafts being sunk two or three hundred feet. Ventilation shafts and drainage tunnels with pumping machines to save the miners from drowning were installed for the first time. The pumps were operated either by water-wheels or by horse-driven machinery. As well as copper mines on this new, big scale, there were tin, silver and lead mines; and the processing industries and associated trades naturally grew on a scale to match the growth of the extraction industries.

Blast-furnaces of a kind introduced from the Continent began to be extensively used in Sussex, still the centre of the iron industry, after about 1540. Before that time iron was produced in small forges manned by manorial tenants under the master-smith, with an output of some-

Alum production from De Re Metallica *by Georgius Agricola, showing:* (a) *the furnace* (b) *enclosed space* (c) *aluminous rock* (d) *deep ladle* (e) *caldron* (f) *launder* (g) *troughs.*

The foundry at Coalbrookdale for the casting of cannon, seen from the Madeley side of the River Severn in Shropshire, 1788.

thing like twenty tons a year. After 1540 the industry was taken up by capitalists and the scale of operations became much larger, not only in Sussex but in Glamorganshire, Monmouthshire, the midlands and the Forest of Dean. Massive square stone towers, thirty feet high, rose all over the iron-fields, with twenty-foot bellows driven by overshot water-wheels nearly thirty feet in diameter, fed by great wooden aqueducts carrying the driving water to a point above the wheel. Around these industrial structures there were furnace houses, bridge-houses to protect the wheels, workmen's hutments and stables for the foundry horses, and the factories, with their giant water-driven hammers, which turned the cast-iron from the furnaces into wrought iron.

These very considerable blast-furnaces, with their complexes of ancillary buildings, were clearly a striking new feature in the scene. Yet even they were not the most striking now added by industry: at Keswick, where skilled workers had been brought over from Germany, copper-mining was combined with copper-smelting and processing and there, in the reign of Charles I, the Society of Mines Royal had an industrial complex so large that its smelting houses alone composed a small town.

Steel was made in small workshops and very small quantities in England in the Middle Ages. Here, too, there were changes which began to make the industry a feature in the landscape. Dutch technicians were brought over to establish relatively large steel-making plants at Robertsbridge in Sussex (1565) and other plants were set up in Kent and Glamorganshire. And factories for the making and cutting of iron bar for nail-making and other trades, and for drawing wire, were set up in the same parts of the country, all powered by water.

So great was the development and expansion of the metal industries at this time, and of the finishing trades associated with them, that the riverside scene in many regions of Britain was quite transformed: on many reaches the ancient quietude was now shattered, and, where there had been no sound but the plop of rising fish and the song of birds, there was now the crash of giant hammers, the regular thump of water-wheels and the sound of many voices. This development was, of course, resented and opposed, and often successsfully, for the government interfered to protect navigation and fishing rights which were thus threatened by industry.

Although the new industries and the developments of the older ones were all accomplished with the help of Huguenot, Dutch and German technicians, by the middle of the seventeenth century England was beginning to overhaul the Continental countries in such works; her

Above: *Iron forging from* De Re Metallica. Below: *An iron mine from an engraving of 1813.*

industries grew faster than theirs despite the Civil War, or perhaps because of it, for wars do stimulate invention and the expansion of the arms industry, producing new techniques and capacities which can later be applied to peaceful manufacture. England was already beginning to be the world's workshop; and already beginning to look like it, to bear, here and there, the terrible but not ignoble stigmata of industry on her face.

The growth of the metal industries, especially iron-founding, ate up the remains of the primeval forests at an alarming pace; so much was this the case that even by the end of Elizabeth's reign the high cost and growing scarcity of firewood was checking industrial expansion. In many industrial processes coal was being substituted for wood, that is for charcoal; but it could not yet be used in the smelting of iron, for its sulphurous fumes spoilt the finished product. Many men in many places were working on this problem, and it was soon to be solved: but meanwhile, by the beginning of the Civil War, the expansion of the iron industry had actually been brought to a halt for want of fuel. At long last England's forests, which had generated themselves all over the country as the ice of the last glacial age retreated, had been destroyed, and the surface of the land lay open to the sun.

It is probable, although not easy to prove, that this destruction of the forests led to a change of great import in the long run: a reduction of the mean annual rainfall, with all its consequences. If that be so, then it was the first climatic change made in Britain by man; and today we are beginning to feel the pinch of it.

Britain was not the only country whose industrial progress was being checked for want of wood; it is true that the shortage was felt in this country before it was felt on the Continent, but on the other hand Britain had an advantage over those countries in one respect: abundance of relatively accessible coal.

Moreover, the English were the first people in history to mine coal on a really vast scale and exploit it to create a great commercial hegemony. They were not the first ever to make use of it, however: the Chinese were using it when Marco Polo was in the Far East and had probably long been doing so, but they dug it only from outcrops, not from deep pits. Moreover, the Romans, when in Britain, made some small use of English coal.

Professor J. U. Nef, the distinguished American historian of our coal industry, rejects the evidence usually cited to prove the post-Roman use of coal before the thirteenth century, while agreeing that there may have been some use of coal and that in any case by 1200 England was exporting a commodity called *charbon de roche* to Bruges. What he really rejects are categorical claims for the existence of coal-mining in Britain at that time, based on documents which can be shown by conscientious scholarship to refer to some other commodity – charcoal, for example. I think we may assume that there was some open-cast coal-digging before 1200, but on a very small scale.

In the thirteenth century open-cast mining began to make small scars on the land's face. By mid-thirteenth century some pits were being dug but they were probably not very deep.

The earliest 'coal-owners' were lay and ecclesiastical lords of the manor; and the first coal-miners were manorial tenants, peasants who spent a part of their time digging coal instead of cultivating the land, as a means of discharging their dues. The pits dug were shaped like inverted cones; as this was the manner in which the Romans dug chalk pits – in the Champagne country, for example – one is entitled to wonder whether the practice might be of Roman origin. The only early pits to yield more than a few tons of coal a year were in the Tyne valley where, by about 1400, there were mines yielding as much as 100 tons a year and perhaps twice as much.

By the fifteenth century coal sufficient to make a significant contribution to manorial revenues was being mined in the Tyne valley, in Glamorganshire, on the river Trent, in the country south of Bishop Auckland in County Durham and also in certain regions of Scotland.

By mid-fourteenth century, Newcastle was exporting coal to the Continent at the rate of between 2,000 and 7,000 tons a year. It cost the merchant seamen who bought it about 2 shillings per ton, was mostly carried in foreign bottoms, and the market for it was so small and uncertain that it was only worth carrying as ballast. Probably about as much coal went to London by coaster as to foreign ports. The principal consumers were blacksmiths and lime-burners, and there was some domestic use; but the smiths were obliged to use it in small quantities mixed with charcoal because coal fumes were apt to spoil the metal.

In short, before the sixteenth century coal-mining did very little to mark Britain's face or retard the rate at which forests were being consumed. But during that century, with wood becoming scarcer and dearer all the time, there was a change.[2]

---

[2] The biggest medieval coalfield in Europe was not in Britain but in Liège whose coal could compete with England's in the Channel and North Sea ports. The Liège miners early

Above: *descent into a coal mine by basket*. Below: *holing the bottom coal, 1878, drawn by John Nash.*

Women workers below ground in Northumberland mines.

The British coalfields being exploited at the beginning of the six-teenth century, however timidly, were those of Durham and Northumberland, South Wales, the midlands, Cumberland and a few small ones elsewhere. By the middle of the century the Durham–Northumberland and the midlands fields were by far the most impor-tant, together providing more than seventy-six per cent of Britain's output; and in those regions appeared the first extensive pitting and scarring of the land's face by coal-mining.

The rash of pitting spread steadily up to the period when coke was discovered; the rate of extension then became much greater. One or two examples: in 1560 the output of coal in the lower Tyne valley was about 35,000 tons a year; a century later it was about half a million tons. Nef gives the trade in coal from Sunderland late in the sixteenth century as not more than 3,000 tons a year; just before the Revolution of 1688,

---

invented coal briquettes which burnt better than small coal. In 1515 eighty miners drowned at Liège owing to the flooding of a mine. See J. U. Nef, *The Rise of the British Coal Industry* (1966).

which finally transferred power from the King to Parliament, it had risen to 180,000 tons. From 1560 to 1690 coal trade from the Northumberland coast rose from 500 to 33,000 tons a year. The story is much the same in other coalfields.

Although some part of this great increase was due to deeper mining (the depth was still limited until the invention of a steam-pump for getting the water out late in the seventeenth century), much of it came from the extension of pit-sinking, with a consequent increase in scarring and rubbish-dumping. One can get an idea of the magnitude of the change in another way: in mid-sixteenth century consumption of coal in England was less than one hundredweight per year per head of the population; by the end of the seventeenth century it was about nine hundredweight per head and the population had increased by perhaps a million.

In Scotland, before the last quarter of the eighteenth century, such coal as was mined was for local use, for want of roads, entailing the use of pack-horses, made export of such bulky stuff impossible. It was easier to import coal from Newcastle, and perhaps even cheaper though there was a duty of 3s. 6d a ton at a time when the price at the port of entry was 4s. 10d (Miller's *Scotch Merchant of the 18th Century*). Scottish coal-miners (and salt-pan workers) were, by an Act of the Scottish Parliament (1606) bound for life to their pit, that is, were made serfs, passing as part of the property to the new pit-owner if the pit were sold. They were compensated by high wages – 2s. 6d a day when (in 1763) the free colliers of Newcastle were paid 1s. a day. Not until 1775 was this Act repealed; and so abominable was the memory of slavery that, when demand for coal made possible the development of the Scottish pits, that development was held back for decades by want of labour.

I have already pointed out that long after coal was replacing wood as fuel it could still not be used for smelting iron because the fumes spoilt the metal. There were other limitations on its use: it could not be used to bake bread, dry malt, make bricks, tiles or pottery; nor to make glass or steel until the closed crucible had been devised.

Various means of getting over this were tried: there were those briquettes made by the Liège colliers, which burnt with less smoke and fumes. In 1603 Sir Hugh Platt, whose principal contributions to justifying God's ways to man were in scientific farming and in beauty culture for ladies, published a recipe for making 'coleballes' of loam and coal-dust which had the same merit. In 1620 the Crown granted a patent for 'charking earth fuel', that is for treating raw coal as charcoal-burners treated wood. Later patents were granted to various people, including a great coal-owning landlord, Sir John Winter, for making what was, more or less, coke; his method is described in John Evelyn's *Diary* (11 July 1656). And in Derbyshire the colliers were already making coke of a kind by using the ancient technique of the charcoal-burner.

Thus the 'invention' of coke can no more be attributed to one man than can the invention of anything else. But the critical advance was made early in the eighteenth century by a Birmingham manufacturer, Abraham Darby, who successfully used his coke for smelting iron-ore.

Darby and his clean coke which, unlike coal, did not spoil the iron in the course of smelting by mixing with it chemical impurities enabled industry to begin forging ahead again, altering more and more of the land's face. Meanwhile, coal was being used for other purposes and, in the process, making more new lines and wrinkles. It or some primitive form of coke was applied to brick-making in the reign of James I, again just in time for the Stuart building boom, which continued throughout the Commonwealth period despite the war, continually raising the demand for bricks. Another advance which affected the building trades and added more industrial buildings to the scene, was made in 1612: a means of closing the clay crucibles, in which sand and potash were fused to make glass, made it possible to use coal instead of wood fuel in the manufacture of sheet-glass and bottles, following which more and larger glass factories were built. This closed-crucible method was applied in 1614 to the making of steel, which, again, stimulated growth in the steel industry.

It has already been mentioned that the manufacture of salt was a very ancient industry in England. In this, too, the substitution of coal for wood as a fuel made new and more striking wrinkles on Britain's face. The method of supply had long been the evaporation of the water from brine-springs in Cheshire and Worcestershire; or of sea-water at various places round the coasts, each region of England having a local source of supply, though there was a national salt centre at Droitwich. It should be remembered that in one respect salt was a more important commodity then than now: it was the only food preservative. The demand for it was continually increasing as population and towns grew larger and the standard of living rose. And there was a very large and increasing demand from the shipping community, both merchant and naval, for the preservation of meat for long voyages.

Above: *Glass blowing in 1747.*

Below: *Ancient method of salt making from* De Re Metallica: (a) *Sea* (b) *port* (c) *gate* (d) *trenches* (e) *salt basins* (f) *rake* (g) *shovel.*

The use of cheap, low-grade coal for heating the salt-pans and evaporating the brine now shifted this very important industry from its old sites to new ones: the mouths of the rivers Tyne and Wear, where the fuel was available, became the new salt-producing district, changing the look of the land with considerable complexes of huge iron pans, twenty feet square and six feet deep, and furnaces, in huge wooden sheds. Even before the end of the sixteenth century as many as 300 men might be employed by a single enterprise; and there was one salt factory at South Shields, at the time of the Civil War, which employed 1,000 men.

Now, too, the factory began to replace the manor and farmhouse still-room and kitchen in brewing and soap-boiling; and the factory complex of kilns replaced the farmstead lime-kiln. For centuries, ale, soap and lime had been produced in thousands of farmsteads, chiefly for home consumption, with the surpluses supplying the towns; the same was true of cider in the west country, the midlands and Kent. For reasons which are not clear, cider long remained a farm industry: it may have had something to do with the fact that no excise duty was ever placed on cider. But in the case of the other three, capitalists saw opportunities for big profits in the rising urban demand, and factory-scale breweries, lime-kilns and soap-boilers were built in many parts of Britain, with the soap industry concentrated in London. Thus these three industries now added their buildings, their rubbish and their coal-smoke to the aspect of the land.

It was doubtless in the reigns of James I and Charles I that Dutch improvements in ship-building began to transform and enlarge British shipyards. There were two technological improvements: the use of big cranes for shifting heavy timbers; and the use of windmills to drive the saws which cut ships' timbers.

These and other changes in the ports and fishing towns of our coasts were stimulated by the sharp and continuous rise in the demand for shipping: first, there was the growth of the Royal Navy; second, the very large and continuing growth in overseas trade; third, the size and number of deep-sea fishing smacks and other types of vessel continued to increase. But there was another cause at work which was, perhaps, even more important than all these. At this time and until the railway age, the best way to move bulky cargoes was by water and, before the canals, this meant by coasting freighters; even as late as Jane Austen's time, when the Dashwoods, in *Sense and Sensibility*, had to move to

Spinning with a distaff.

Devonshire from the home counties, their heavy furniture was sent by sea. But the practice was an extremely ancient one: the Pembrokeshire stones for the building of Stonehenge can only have been moved by sea. So the growth of ship-building yard complexes, and of hundreds of ports, small and large, was stimulated by the coasting carrier trade. Between the end of the fourteenth century and the Civil War, the weight of coal carried by coasters from Tynemouth to Thames-side increased from 30,000 tons a year to about half a million tons.

So our coastal profile was changed by the growth of ports and harbours; and by the number of shipyards in estuaries, which were once the haunt of coot and tern, building more and bigger ships.

For many centuries Britain exported her wool and imported her cloth. We tend to think nowadays of our country as an importer of raw materials for manufacturing and finishing for export. But I have already said that she was the medieval Australia, a primary, not a secondary, producer. Sheep, not textile mills, were the striking feature in that time of the 'textile landscape'.

When we did begin to knit our own stockings, to make worsteds, cotton goods and linens, the industry was in farmhouses and cottages: not for nothing was an unmarried woman called a spinster, though that designation is not fair to the housewives who were quite as active in spinning despite having the house and children to look after. At first, of course, the yarn spun and the cloth woven in farmhouse and cottage was for domestic use. Tradesmen turned it into an industry by paying the spinsters, housewives and weavers (men as well as women) for what they could make over and above what they needed at home, and selling it in the towns. And something like this pattern endured long beyond the period we are here concerned with.

But the factories were being built early in the eighteenth century for the finishing processes: for dyeing, fulling and calendering. Britain became a dangerous competitor of the Low Countries in the exporting of finished cloth from these factories, the more dangerous in that the clothiers were given every kind of government aid in the service of that 'mercantilism' which held that the country's industry and commerce should be used as political weapons: not only was the textile industry protected against imports by duties or bans on imported cloth; but there was even a law providing for the burial of the dead in woollen shrouds and for the prevention of emigration of skilled craftsmen.

So the textile industry, too, began to change the face of the country, although the dark, satanic mills had yet to appear.

The year 1760 is commonly taken as the starting point of that great spurt in industrial evolution which is usually called the Industrial Revolution. What gave rise to that acceleration is not really our subject: the Renaissance-born spirit of curiosity turning to practical physics and chemistry; surplus capital seeking investment; surplus labour seeking work and wages; more, and more accessible, raw materials; wider markets, better communications; a new respect for the practical mechanic and for trade, all these and many other things were factors; above all, the mastery of steam power.

There were, for example, very considerable textile factories in the Lancashire and Yorkshire hill country, and in Lanarkshire, where water-power was available, using Arkwright's water frame invented in 1769 but still bound to the riverside by the need for a powerful and reliable flow of water to drive the machinery. Steam-power broke that bond; it was steam which transformed Glasgow and Paisley and a score of other small towns into great cities; you could build a steam engine anywhere, though in practice you built it where there was the coal to generate steam in order to eliminate the heavy cost of carrying fuel. Which is why so much of Britain's industry is in the coalfields.

The first workable steam-engine was constructed by the Marquis of Worcester in 1663; Papin took it a stage further in 1690; in 1698 Savery started to use an improved version of Papin's engine to pump water out of mines. That was the only use for the engine until Watt and Murdoch made it impart rotary motion to a wheel. But Newcomen improved

Savery's machine; James Watt improved Newcomen's or, rather, Smeaton's modification of it. Watt's much improved engine was working by 1769, the year of Arkwright's invention of the water-frame. The Cornish mine-engineer Trevithick, and another inventor, Hornblower, made some contributions. And at last James Watt, financed first by John Roebuck, later by Matthew Boulton, and helped by Boulton's very able foreman, William Murdoch, himself the builder of an early locomotive and the first man to use coal-gas for lighting, found a way to make their engine impart rotary motion to a wheel (1781). This refinement gave the industrialists the tool they needed.

That all but one of the names in the above paragraph will be unknown to most readers does not matter: the object of describing the 'invention' of the steam-engine in that way is to make it clear that there was indeed, no 'revolution', and that 'evolution' is a truer word in this context.

Within a few years, then, began that development and expansion of steam-powered industry which put such huge and hideous scars on those parts of the land's face where coal was to be found: the Tyne Basin, Britain's oldest coalfield; south Lancashire; west Yorkshire; the Staffordshire Black Country; the Forth and Clyde Valleys and north and south Wales.

Acceleration of the process of industrialization was a product of mutual stimulation between industries:

The coal and iron trades are inseparably connected. In various ways each acted and reacted on the other. Each advance in the mining of coal made possible a greater output of pig-iron; every improvement in the iron trade called forth a speeding up in the production of coal, and out of these co-related developments sprang most of the new industries with which England had provided herself by 1850.[3]

So more and more of Britain's green and fragrant skin was covered with grimy masonry, huge heaps of slag, streets of cottages built to minimal standards for miners and mill operatives. This growth was never planned, never foreseen, was, in a sense, organic. Each mine and factory surrounded itself with a repulsive mess that added to the scarring; but managements did not think of themselves as spoiling the country's face; their own contribution to ugliness would have looked very tiny on a map of Britain, even had they given a moment's thought to it, which

---

[3] M. Briggs and P. Jordan, *Economic History of England*. London, 1960.

they surely never did. This was the visual price of industrial progress; to wonder now whether that progress was a good or bad thing is beside the point; it was the product of a process in which momentum was self-generating. The ruin of large tracts of countryside by early industry was as inevitable as the ruin of a countryside by volcanic eruption, for not only was the idea of 'planning' not yet conceived, it would have been anathema.

The application of steam-power to industry produced an intellectual and moral climate stimulating to invention. I think it will be clear from the paragraph above dealing with the evolution of the steam-engine itself, that there is not too great an abuse of words in alling that, also, an 'organic' growth. For some reason it is satisfying to think of invention as a kind of brain-wave in the mind of a genius, or as the brilliant and beautiful conclusion to a long train of logical thought in one man's mind. And that is how it appears in industrial and scientific folk-lore. But this image is so remote from the truth that, the more obstinately one tries to discover who invented what, the clearer it becomes that when we say, for example, that Marconi invented radio or Darwin the theory of evolution by natural selection, what we mean is that a particular man was the first who made a practical use or a clear statement of an idea which had grown little by little through a long series of minds.

The geographically concentrating effect of the use of steam-power in industry produced the most extreme visual changes in particular regions. While the textile industries, for example, remained manual, domestic trades, they were very widely dispersed all over Britain. With water-power they were less so, because you could not have a mill without a fast-flowing stream – hence the establishment of those industries in, for instance, the Pennines. But still there was no intensive localization. With steam, the cotton industry became concentrated in southern Lancashire, the woollen trade in Yorkshire's West Riding, almost vanishing from East Anglia, Norfolk, Gloucestershire, Devonshire and Wiltshire. In both cases, coal was the magnet, although there were some other causes also. So, textiles, too, spread a rash of buildings in its least beautiful manifestation, like a grey acne over those two regions.

Typical of this concentrating effect of coal was the case of the iron_masters. It was now that firms whose names have remained famous in the industry began to migrate to the coalfields: the Guests, Hornfrays and others from Shropshire to south Wales; the Parkers from Coalbrookdale to Tipton; the Williamses from Ludlow to Wednesbury; Thorneycrofts from Broseley to Wolverhampton, the Carron

Typical miners' cottages, photographed in 1973.

Ironworks – casters of the eponymous 'carronade' guns – to Falkirk, and so forth.

These developments, then, all depended on more and more coal: it was fuel for furnaces; it was coke for smelting; and with the rise of a chemical industry, it was an important raw material from which many things could be extracted, as it was also the source of gas for lighting.

The mess made by pre-steam-age mining was insignificant. For one thing, the depth of mines, and therefore the amount of slag and such rubbish brought from the depths, was very limited. The practice was first to get out the coal near the surface, then to sink shafts to the seam below, work that out, and go down again, but to continue this process only for as long as the topography (British coal is mostly in hilly districts) made it possible for galleries to open into the air and so to be drained of water and gases. Before steam-pumping, the miners could not with any safety go much deeper than that, because they were apt to be drowned in the water which accumulated, by percolation, in the undrained bottom of the mine.

Steam-pumping allowed for deeper mines, greatly increased production, and therefore greatly extended the areas of scarring and rubbish-dumping. At first there were few other improvements in technique to forward this process: mine roofs, for example, were still supported by leaving pillars of coal in the cutting until about 1810 when wooden pit-props were introduced. This single improvement in mining technique alone produced two new changes in the land's face: it speeded the destruction of forest, although much of the pit-prop timber had to be imported; and, in due course, stimulated the introduction of coniferous soft-wood species of trees, larch and spruce, and ultimately their planting on such a vast scale that it caused an outcry among those who thought that the wholly imaginary 'immemorial' face of Britain was being disfigured by these arborial aliens. Five years later came the Davy safety lamp; underground mechanical haulage in 1820; steam-driven boring machines and winding machines in 1830; the iron cage in 1835; the use of iron wire ropes in 1840; steam-driven ventilation in 1850; the first mechanized coal cutters in 1861.

Thus very deep mining became first practicable and finally easy, although shallow and surface mining long remained the rule in south Wales and in coalfields south of Durham in England. Deep or shallow, the scarring of Britain's surface and the rash of slag heaps and rubbish tips became more and more hideous, and hundreds of square miles of the land's face were disfigured.

There were many places where the rate of scarring, the pace at which the rash of ugly buildings and rubbish tips spread, was much faster because coal lay alongside other minerals. The ancient English ironfield was the Weald; but the new ones lay beside the coalfields in England, Scotland and south Wales, a great stroke of luck for industry but something of a disaster for the locality's beauty. Thus, the best iron-ore, occurring in large nodules which lay in seams, like coal, was found near Bradford, and iron-ore beside the coalfields in the Clyde and Forth Valleys.

The spoiling of the rural beauty of Britain, inevitable consequence of industrial expansion, had begun.

9   The Netted Skin

Few things have made greater changes in the aspect of Britain than the transport networks laid down on to her skin, one after another. From the air they are like an elaborate reticulation, like the network of wrinkles on an old woman's face.

The first means of inland transport used by men in England was that of the rivers, and the more readily navigable ones have remained important. Although, as we have seen, the Romans gave the land a system of roads, and although parts of it were restored and used by the Saxons who, during the epoch of village-founding, beat out new ones with their wandering feet, as did the new English after them, yet until the sixteenth and even into the seventeenth century rivers were still the most important of the common highways. And not even the king could legally prevent any man from using them. So true is this that when the growth of industry set water-wheels and weirs in the way of river navigation, it was navigation which had the priority in law, so that industrialists were often hampered in their development. In Tudor times there were several Acts of Parliament compelling industrialists to remove such obstructions.

This navigational importance of rivers itself led to some changes on the face of Britain, as deeper channels were dredged and reaches of certain rivers embanked. Locks appeared along the courses of some rivers, and as these were often in reaches flowing through private estates, tolls were charged for using them. But such changes were, on the whole, rather minor ones and are not much to our purpose. Still, man's works changed the course of rivers, forced shallow, spreading waters into deep embanked streams, eliminated marshes and crowded long reaches of the riverside with masonry.

In the Middle Ages roads were the responsibility of land-owners who were obliged by law to keep them in order. The great monastic land-owners were fairly conscientious in fulfilling this duty; but their succes-

Medieval transport from the Luttrel Psalter.

sors, who held English estates following the Dissolution of the Monasteries, were not; their motto was not service but profit. Consequently, new laws became necessary.

A number of Acts of Parliament made the parish responsible for the roads (1555, 1562, 1573); this was a transport disaster of great magnitude, since it became impossible to deal with roads on a national scale and, for centuries, the badness of British roads became a byword. Moreover, the system of getting labour for road-work, although splendid in theory, did not work in practice: every householder was legally obliged to contribute six days' work a year to the labour of maintaining and making roads. A householder could do this duty either in his own person, or by paying a substitute, but even so the *corvée* was evaded on an enormous scale. There were parishes where the roads were well maintained but in others, perhaps in the majority, they were so bad as to be frequently impassable and even dangerous: there is a story of two men standing on a roadside bank who observed a gentleman's hat moving, apparently of its own accord, along the muddy surface of the miry road; on investigating this strange phenomenon they found that there was a gentleman on horseback under the hat. An exaggeration, no doubt; but a significant one. In Scotland, Wales and Cornwall the 'highways' were tracks of mud or sheets of ice in winter. The Scots were obliged to use pack-horses even in the neighbourhood of Edinburgh until late in the eighteenth century. Until 1786 there was only one coach per month from Edinburgh to London and the journey took a fortnight. A Glaswegian wishing to go to London could either go by sea, which might, in foul weather, take a month; or ride to Newcastle and there take a place on the eight-horse wagon which did the journey in eighteen days.

With the rise of industrial capitalism came the notion that the people who used the roads should pay for them, a principle still maintained in our own vehicle licences, originally called Road Fund licences, and in the toll motorways of Italy, France and the United States. So the so-called Turnpike System came into existence, the first Turnpike Trust being formed in 1663 to improve the main road through Hertfordshire, Cambridgeshire and Huntingdonshire. Tolls were charged, county justices were empowered to appoint professional road surveyors paid, as were the road labourers, out of toll revenues. Until 1706, the turnpikes were all authorized by Public Acts of Parliament, thereafter by Private Acts with bodies of Trustees administering the road.

This system added many hundreds of miles of new road, and its benefits are best expressed in examples contrasting with those above: two coaches per day plied from Edinburgh to London, and cut the journey time from fourteen days to sixty hours. The Glasgow to London journey time was cut from anything up to a month, to sixty-five hours in one of Palmer's famous coaches. But we should take the system's many defects into account, since to some extent they gave the road network its particular shape. It was not, G. K. Chesterton notwithstanding, the rolling English drunkard who made the rolling English road; it was, even less creditably, the self-interest of rich and influential land-owners, often themselves road commissioners or trustees, who decided the course that new roads should take to suit their own interests, without regard to the surveyor's choice of route. Thus roads went zigzag which should have gone straight, or went over hills with impossible gradients, instead of going round them. The turnpike roads network was thus dictated not by the need for the best possible system of communications rationally interpreted by experienced engineers, but by the whims, fancies, prejudices and selfishness of many thousands of interested parties. When, today, we spend millions in straightening roads, we are wiping from the face of England an expression of human nature.

As industry developed with the provision of steam-power, and the increasing tonnages of its products had to be moved by road, the turnpike system, with its hundreds of different bodies of administrators all with different standards and methods of maintenance, and with no uniformity of road for more than a dozen or so miles at a stretch, was revealed as ever more inadequate. A number of Acts aimed at improving roads were passed between 1770 and 1835. They were not very effective. When, a few decades later, the competition of railways so reduced revenues from tolls that there was not enough money even for basic road

Above: *The Archway over the Great North Road, built by Thomas Telford and opened to traffic in 1813. Tolls of a few pence, according to the vehicle, were levied at the bottom of the hill where the New Road joined Highgate Hill.* Below: *The toll gate in 1860. It was made public in 1876.*

maintenance, the system collapsed and had to be abolished. If, today, France and the United States, both richer than Britain, and Italy whose economy is in no worse a state, have toll motorways, whereas our own are free, it is at least in part because the abuse of turnpike franchises left such a bad taste in British mouths.

But the turnpike system also produced some outstanding road engineers who did lay down roads on rational topographical principles and with proper regard to the convenience of road-users. They thereby added lines of greater beauty to the country's facial network, and laid the foundation of a good road system which was to be required when the perfection of the internal combustion engine turned the tables on the railways. In some ways the most remarkable was Metcalfe, 'Blind Jack of Knaresborough', whose work was done in the second half of the eighteenth century; he studied, with hands and feet, since he could not see, the geology and topography of the country where the road was to be built, wound his roads about to use the main valleys and so keep gradients low, pioneered the building of roads over soft and even boggy land, and made use of cuttings. Then there was Thomas Telford (1757–1834), who was the first road engineer to pay proper attention to making a good surface, to efficient subsoil drainage, and to the degree of camber to give the best surface drainage.

Telford was the son of a shepherd, who educated himself as an engineer and road surveyor. His first major work was the building of a three-arch bridge over the Severn at Shrewsbury. Before his death he had designed about 1,200 road bridges and built over 100, the grandest being the world-famous suspension bridge which joined Anglesey to the mainland. Among his roads were the Shrewsbury to Holyhead and the Chester to Bangor; in all he added about 1,000 miles of road to the national network. Like 'Blind Jack of Knaresborough' he insisted on a low gradient, setting as a limit a rise of one in thirty. He used stone blocks as foundation for his roads, broken rock, pebbles or gravel for the surfaces. Telford's roads reflected the geology of the land through which they passed, for he always used local materials when he could; this meant that the quality of the roads varied greatly from place to place, but only occasionally could he persuade turnpike trustees to go to the expense of importing better materials than their parish afforded. He made use of unusual materials on some occasions: he discovered that the slag from copper foundries made a good road surface.

The most famous name in road-making is still Macadam's. John Loudon Macadam (175–1836), a Scottish civil engineer, was appointed surveyor to the Bristol District of Roads in 1815. Unlike Telford, he preferred a soft foundation, holding that surface wear was much less above a soft than above a hard basis. Like Telford's, his roads were eighteen feet wide, but he did not like a steep camber, finding that where the surface was good a difference of only three inches from the edge to the centre was sufficient to ensure surface drainage. His book, *The Present System of Road-making*, became the road engineer's handbook. He was so particular about using stones of a standard size for surfacing that he made his surveyors carry scales and a six-ounce weight to weigh a random sample of the stones from each heap provided by his gangs of male and female stone-breakers. His method was to lay a six-inch depth of these stones, let them settle and traffic consolidate them for some weeks, and then put another six inches on top of them. Italian motorway engineers still use this method of consolidation by traffic before finishing. His work was thus responsible for a great increase in the rate of stone-quarrying, so that he was marking the face of England in more ways than one. His road-building method became known as macadamizing and it was adopted for turnpikes all over Britain.

By mid-nineteenth century the network of public roads in Britain measured about 105,000 miles, 22,000 of these being macadamized turnpike. There were, however, many country districts where only the bare minimum of road maintenance and no road building had been done for centuries and where the cross-country roads were still appalling.

A network of new lines of quite another kind was dug into Britain's face between 1760 and 1830: the inland waterways or canals.

They were called into existence by need: as industry developed and spread over wider areas of Lancashire and Yorkshire, the Welsh valleys and those of Forth and Clyde, the population grew at an ever increasing pace. None of these industrial regions could produce enough food locally to feed such large populations; and it was so difficult to carry enough food into them by pack-horse and wagon over bad roads, that there were often serious winter shortages. Because of the same transport difficulties, even coal prices were far too high. It was the Duke of Bridgewater who decided to link Manchester to Liverpool by waterway, digging a canal from his Worsley coal-mines to Salford and from Salford to Runcorn. Fortunately the man for his purpose was to hand; in fact, it was this engineer of genius, James Brindley (1716–72), a Derbyshire man, who first suggested the canal to the Duke.

Above: *Manoeuvring barges into a lock on the Grand Union Canal a few miles out of Watford, off the road to Kings Langley, Hertfordshire.* Below: *the northern entrance of the Harecastle tunnels on the Grand Trunk Canal at Brindley.*

Following the success of this first inland waterway, there was a boom in canal-cutting. Thousands of labourers, many of them Irish, swarmed out over the land, digging and embanking, bringing uproar into quiet country parishes, and gangs of rough aliens into the new industrial towns. Because they were digging navigation canals, they were known as 'navigators', hence 'navvies'. The face of England was dug, bored and tunnelled by these navvies, the pace of the work being forwarded by fierce rivalry between gangs. The promotion of canal projects became a speculative bonanza, and while most of the schemes put forward were practical enough, there were ridiculous ones, such as projects to cut a second canal alongside an existing one, to compete with it. Once again, there was no national plan, no national authority, but a confused muddle of enterprises, large and small, which resulted in inefficiently surveyed courses, maldistribution of carrying capacity and enormous waste of resources, all the usual evils of unrestrained capitalism.

The making of inland waterways added more than hundreds of miles of canals to the land's face. Brindley, for example, had to carry his Bridgewater Canal over the Orwell valley in a great aqueduct. Telford, the great bridge-builder and road engineer, in charge of the Ellesmere Canal, built two superb aqueducts, one at Chirk and the second over the river Dee. And, of course, there were thousands of locks to be built.

The Grand Trunk Canal, linking Liverpool to the midlands and to Hull, was soon carrying Cheshire salt and Staffordshire pottery to their markets. It linked to London and Bristol by more canal-cutting; Leeds was connected by waterway to Liverpool; canals were dug to carry Birmingham's ironware all over the country and to the ports of export, and foodstuffs and raw materials into Birmingham. The east and west of Scotland were opened to each other by the Forth and Clyde Canal. As well as locks and aqueducts, pumping stations to raise huge volumes of water were new features on the face of the land. It became possible to carry china-clay by barge from Cornwall to the Staffordshire potteries, coal from the mining districts to all their markets and ports of export, food into all the regions of proliferating industry, and their manufactured goods out again.

The network of inland waterways had a secondary effect in changing the look of the land. It enabled industrialists to site new factories away from the towns, since the cost of carriage of all necessary materials and of finished products was now very much lower and could easily be absorbed. So industrial scenery began to spread out from the great centres along the canal courses, and bricks and mortar replaced grass

Telford's Chirk Aqueduct.

and trees, the clamour of machinery broke the rural silence. Another point is worth noting: a single horse drawing a barge could do the work of very many horses carrying packs or dragging wagons. During the canal-building era this was taken to mean that, since it took six acres to grow enough food to feed one cart-horse, there would now be a great saving in the amount of land required to grow hay, so that more land would be available for the growing of corn and other food-crops for men. And it is likely enough that for a time this by-product of the canal-cutters' work was a reality, and that the face of agricultural England bore a changed aspect. But certainly not for long: canals could not carry goods and materials everywhere; the continuous expansion of industry requiring more and more transport produced such an increase in the horse-population that demand for hay became greater than ever and grass-growing engrossed more land than ever before in England's history.[1]

As well as the canals for barge traffic, ship canals made changes in England's aspect. The first was the Exeter canal, long since too shallow for big ships although Telford deepened it once after it had been cut. The Manchester Ship Canal, by far the most important, was cut between 1887 and 1894: beginning at the Mersey estuary, it was tidal sea-water to the first lock near Warrington, then fresh water to Manchester. As this mighty canal had to cross James Brindley's old canal, its engineer, Sir E. Leader Williams, here built something entirely new to the English scene, a swing aqueduct which could be swung aside to let tall ships pass.

This great ship canal made a considerable change in Britain's industrial topography: Manchester, an inland city, was transformed into a great seaport; Liverpool suffered a considerable loss of importance.

The third network of new lines laid on England's face was, of course, the railways. This process began in the sixteenth century when railways made of wooden rails were laid, on which trains of wagons could be drawn by horses from, for example, the Newcastle mines to Tyneside for shipment to London and the Continent. Iron rails were first used for a similar horse-railway at Coalbrookdale in 1767. And the first steam locomotive was used on such a railway at Merthyr Tydfil, by the Cornish engineer Trevithick, in 1804. Then came 'Puffing Billy' used on the mine railway near Wylam in 1811; and Stephenson's first engine three years later.

To revert for a moment to the road network: the need for the work of such men as Metcalfe, Telford and Macadam was, of course, the need for fast transport of passengers, and reliable transport of freight as population and industry grew; but it is also true to say that their work stimulated the more rapid growth of those kinds of road transport, and made possible the development of the splendid system of stage-coach

[1] M. Briggs and P. Jordan, *Economic History of England*. London, 1960.

Above: *the Manchester Ship Canal, showing the Barten aqueduct carrying the Bridgewater Canal over it.* Below: *Saltash Bridge in the nineteenth century.*

communication, carrying mail and passengers, as well as the system of freight carriage by heavy wagons. Thus, by the time Stephenson's first engine was puffing busily out of its shed, there were very powerful interests vested in the stage-coach business and, of course, in the continuing prosperity of turnpike companies. Predictably, they fought the growth of railways with every means they could find.

To anticipate for a moment, by the 1830s there were 3,000 coaches on the roads, using 150,000 horses and about 30,000 men – coachmen, guards, horse-keepers and ostlers. These figures represent a very large investment and the reaction of the interested parties was bitter.

A striking instance of the bitterness which marked the early years of the struggle is provided by a poster published in 1843 by the stage-coach proprietors in northern England whose trade was threatened by the expansion of the Leeds and Manchester railway. The poster headed 'Lies and the Manchester Railway' parodied a railway announcement and set out the 'striking advantages' which travellers could enjoy on 'our magnificent and splendid railway'. Referred to the railway's promise to increase the speed of travelling, the poster pointed out that 'as this will augment the danger, and increase the number of casualties, we have arranged that cemeteries shall be immediately erected at each station, and plans for such cemeteries deposited for passengers previously to starting, to book a place in, by payment of a small charge, so that when the accidents happen, there will be no confusion or unpleasantness in the arrangement for the burial of bodies. A dissecting room will be attached.'[2]

How much more entertaining our own advertising would be if competing interests had not agreed to scratch each other's backs instead of blacking each other's eyes. However, this poster demonstrates the sort of difficulties the railways had to cope with, not to mention the opposition of many land-owners to such changes in the look of their land as the railways must surely bring about.

Stephenson began building the Stockton to Darlington railway in 1825. It was built to carry coal; and when completed it brought the price of coal crashing down from 18s. to 8s. a ton. The point was made; and Stephenson was commissioned to build his second railway from Liverpool to Manchester; it was opened to traffic in 1830, the first train being drawn by his famous 'Rocket' locomotive.

More railways were soon being built and between 1840 and 1850 railway promoting and building became a mania, as canal-cutting had been but on a much bigger scale, with nation-wide speculation in railway shares culminating in a serious financial crisis in 1847. By 1850 a network of 6,600 miles of line had been laid on Britain's face, and it was

[2] J. Copeland, *Roads and Their Traffic 1750–1850*. London, 1968.

George Stephenson's 'Rocket'.

still growing and spreading fast, so that by 1870 it had reached 15,000 miles. The great engineers of this new feature in the land's face were Stephenson, of course, in the north; Isambard Kingdom Brunel, whose broad-gauge Great Western was an immense advance; Cubitt of the Great Northern; and John Hawkshaw in London and the south-east.

The railway builders made a far greater change in the aspect of Britain than that of adding tens of thousands of iron rails, embankments, cuttings, tunnels, stations and bridges to the scene. Towns grew into big cities because the railway was there to feed them with raw materials and carry away their manufactures. Towns came into existence simply to serve the railways: Swindon, for example.

The **Great Eastern** *under repairs on the Cheshire shore of the River Mersey.*

Cities already large now grew at a fantastic pace, spreading and sprawling to cover hundreds of square miles of what had been open country: London, Birmingham, Manchester, Carlisle and Peterborough are a few examples. The Peterborough example is particularly interesting: the London–Carlisle–Glasgow line of the Great Northern was to have run through Stamford but the very powerful stage-coach interest there, and the influence of the Cecils (see p. 207), were able to prevent it. Peterborough was chosen as the best alternative and as a result began to grow in importance as Stamford declined. Moreover, the railways created a very large new demand for coal and iron, forcing expansion on those industries which therefore took up more and more room on the land's face.

And since steamship building was also making great progress at the same time – Brunel, builder of the Great Western railway, built the *Great Western* and the *Great Eastern*, the first two giant ocean liners –

At the launching of the Great Eastern *in 1857,* left to right, *Henry Wakefield, Isambard Kingdom Brunel and Mark Darby.*

the increased growth of export and import trade stimulated a similar growth in a whole range of industries.

Because, also, of that growth in sea-borne trade, the growth of the ports played an important part in creating the man-made face of Britain. There would be little point in describing the development of each major port; but as the port of London was and is the greatest, it will be worth following a sketch of its growth and seeing how it overwhelmed such a vast territory of wilderness England.

It will be remembered that London is sited where it is because it was the first point, on the way inland from the river mouth, at which the river could be crossed by a ford, a fact due to a seam of firm gravel which crosses the river's course at that point. The ford was important to traders because goods landed at the Channel ports and destined for the rich market of East Anglia, had to be carried over the river into Essex.

Then it became obvious, as merchant seamen learnt some more geography, that it would be better to carry the goods in and out of the country by the mouth of the Thames. Thus the settlement of London began to grow into a town based on a trading port. In 1975 archaeologists found evidence of occupation at least 5,000 years old; and Bronze Age artefacts suggesting a settlement on high ground, below where St Paul's now stands, on the north bank of the river. 'Village' London may be as ancient as 'Village' Rome; and surely its port was its nucleus.

This port, in turn, began to grow when the Romans rebuilt London using stone and brick as well as timber, although it had considerable importance some decades before the Claudian conquest. It was from London that such Celtic British exports as slaves, hides and skins, gold, silver and copper, and hunting-dogs, went to the Continent; and into London that foreign traders sent such manufactured goods as pottery and glass and such luxuries for the Belgic chiefs as wine.

By A.D. 61 the port of London was considerable enough for Tacitus to report it as 'much frequented by a number of merchants and trading vessels'. But what did it look like? Not, certainly, like the great stone and marble harbours of the Mediterranean built on models established by Greek architects at least as early as the fourth century B.C. There was a small town with a few stone buildings, temples for example; one or two buildings of brick, that thin Roman brick so nicely accommodated to the small Italian hand; for the most part the houses were of timber, a huddle of modest dwellings backed by marsh, and the woodland on rising ground: a rustic harbour on the outskirts of the known world.

Ships from the Continental ports moored in midstream and their cargoes were unloaded into small boats, that is by lighterage, a method which lasted for more than a thousand years in London's rivers. But the little Roman town had colossal potential importance for the future, from it the Roman roads radiated all over England, and to it they came from the Channel ports, as the tracks of prehistoric traders had done.

During the Roman centuries, that little natural harbour formed by the junction of the Thames, Fleet and Walbrook rivers was provided with wooden jetties and some stone quays. Gradually the wide and shallow stream was crowded in upon by building, forced to flow between artificial banks, ultimately embanked, so that it grew, with the help, in due course, of some dredging, deeper and narrower, and withdrew from its marshes into a channel which could carry ships of deep draught. Ships could lay alongside, though lighterage continued to be

A Roman barge, found at Blackfriars in 1963.

the chief means of handling cargoes. But the time was coming fast when Roman military officers and civil servants, posted to this dreary outpost of empire might not be quite so depressed as they had expected to be when they left home, at the aspect of the city which Rome had built for these northern savages. For by the middle of the fourth century it was possible to describe London and her port as a great and wealthy city (if you were not familiar with Rome, say, or Alexandria). And there was something in it, for by then no fewer than 800 cargoes of grain went annually from her port to the Rhine grain silos, not to mention all the other cargoes.

What happened to the port and city after the withdrawal of the Legions (408) is not documented; there are almost no clues for the next two centuries. However, the city was certainly not abandoned, and trade into and out of its port continued. According to the Anglo-Saxon Chronicle it was to London that the Romano-Britons fled when defeated by the Saxons under Hengist and Ese at Crayford. There was a bishop of London at least as early as 604, and the Venerable Bede describes it as 'the 'metropolis of the East Saxons' and 'a mart of many nations resorting to it by sea and land'. It is very likely that the walls and the port installations were maintained.

Danish sea-raiding between about 800 and 1000 enhanced the city's importance as a strong refuge, easily defensible and as a great warehouse; it now also became the most considerable port of construction, building Saxon warships to fight the Danish pirates; such ships became merchantmen when there was no fighting to be done and Saxon London merchants took to the import-export trade with enthusiasm. So even at this difficult time the port of London was growing, engrossing more and more of the water-meadows and marshy land beside the river. King Alfred gave river-front land to Archbishop Ethelred specifically for dock extension and the Archbishop built Ethelredhithe (hithe means a wharf) which later became Queenhithe. Quays at the same site just above Southwark Bridge are still in use for handling cargoes.

The port of London already had fixed regulations, with a scale of harbour tolls charged to vessels from the various Continental ports. The development of Billingsgate as a hithe belongs to the ninth century. Then, during Canute's reign London became the Danish naval headquarters and increased its ship-building activities, so that docks continued to spread along the north bank.

An influence which increased London's importance as a port in Norman times, and so speeded the pace at which docks and wharves spread up and down river, was that of the Easterlings, German traders and seamen who, in the twelfth century, founded the Hanse, that league of free merchant cities which dominated sea-borne trade for some centuries. The League's London headquarters, later known as the Steelyard, was where Cannon Street Station now stands, and the Hanse wharves lay along the Thames south of the Steelyard. Then, in 1390, came Richard II's Navigation Law which required that English cargoes be exported only in English ships; this stimulated ship-building and more yards spread along the river banks.

The rate at which the port grew can be estimated, roughly, from the records of chartered trading companies. Thus, it was from Deptford that Hugh Willoughby and Richard Chancellor sailed to open up trade with Russia in 1553, acting for a syndicate which two years later became the Russia Company. It was from Woolwich that the first venture of the new East India Company sailed in 1601. There was still green, open country between these dock areas, and between them and the docks within London itself, but steadily the elements of the great port grew towards each other, ultimately to enclose the deepening stream between walls of masonry instead of meadows. By about the middle of Elizabeth's reign one half of England's total customs revenue was collected in London. And meanwhile Southampton, second in importance, was also growing, as were both Newcastle and Bristol, under the same stimulating pressures: Liverpool and Cardiff had yet to become important ports but Glasgow was growing fast: between 1750, when it was known as a very pretty and orderly little town of twenty thousand people, set among green hills and rich farmland, and 1800, the population quadrupled, largely as a result of the growth of the port on the rum and tobacco trade with Virginia, Maryland and the West Indies. The American Revolution ruined that trade; but the growth of the port soon began again, first on the sugar importing trade, then on cotton for the spinning-mills, calico printers and muslin-weavers. Each new industry – coal, iron, steel machinery, chemicals – tended to enlarge the port, transforming more and more miles of green and pleasant littoral into wharves, warehouses and ship-building yards.

When, in 1558, a Royal Commission designated a number of wharves as 'legal quays' at which foreign ships or ships carrying cargoes from overseas were obliged to unload – the measure was to ensure the collection of customs duties which were being evaded on a grand scale – no fewer than twenty wharves had to be chosen, all of them between London Bridge (built in 1209) and the Tower. These twenty wharves

Above: *the hall and warehouse of the Hanseatic League of Merchants at the Steelyard in the City of London. Although expelled by Queen Elizabeth, they continued trading.* Below: *the coat of arms of the Hanseatic League, cut in stone. It was taken down when the Steelyard was demolished in 1863, and is now in the Guildhall Museum.*

soon proved inadequate to the volume of trade and more wharves (known as 'Sufferance quays') had to be designated, after such men as Sir Thomas Gresham set out to make London the commercial and financial capital of Europe, and after the Duke of Parma's vicious folly in sacking Antwerp gave London the chance to replace the Flemish port as the predominant port of transhipment and the greatest *entrepôt*.

The East India Company built the first London dock which had gates at Blackwall. This was not for handling cargoes, for those had to be unloaded by lighter on to one of the 'legal quays', but for the fitting out of ships built in the big Blackwall building yard. At about the same time a new chartered company, the Hudson's Bay Company, added new docks and wharves to the riverside scene.

The Great Fire in 1666 did the port of London a service, however disastrous it must have seemed at the time, by destroying virtually all the old wharf and warehouse accommodation (and, no doubt, thousands of plague-bearing rats), making rebuilding necessary, a chance to re-equip the port on more rational and commodious lines. The work was financed by giving the port authorities a share of the special tax of 1s. on every chaldron of coal entering the port of London, levied to pay for the rebuilding of the city.

At the end of the seventeenth century the ten-acre Howland Great Wet Dock at Rotherhithe was added to the riverside complex; it was the start and nucleus of the Surrey Commercial Docks system. Such expansion was made almost continuously necessary by the number of new kinds of cargo being added all the time to the commerce of the port – sugar, rum, dyewoods, ginger and such luxuries, as well as an ever increasing volume of necessities.

Such growth during the eighteenth century was sporadic, but very considerable: volume of trade through the port doubled between 1700 and 1770, doubled again between 1770 and 1795 by which year imports into London's river exceeded £12 million a year, exports £15 million. These sums must be multiplied by a factor of more than twenty to get any idea of the value of this trade in our money. By this time the port had become appallingly congested: instead of the 545 ships which could comfortably be handled simultaneously, it usually had about three times that number loading and unloading by means of 3,500 lighters, and traffic jams were such that ships could hardly make their way down river to the sea. Wharf proprietors were coining money and fought strenuously to prevent the building of more wharves. After several abortive attempts to deal with this situation, in 1799 Parliament authorized the

Above: *The demolition of old London Bridge, as it appeared in 1832.*

Below: *Howland Great Wet Dock.*

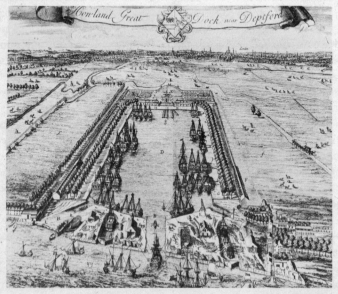

building of new docks on the Isle of Dogs, by the West India Company. So docks and a range of five-storey warehouses, surrounded by high walls manned by 100 armed guards, made necessary by the activities of armed gangs of thieves which infested the port, replaced the woods and meadows of the island.

A canal was cut from Limehouse Reach to Blackwall Reach to bypass the congested channels round the Isle of Dogs. It failed financially, and was transformed into a timber dock, later enlarged to become the South West India Dock. Meanwhile more docks were being built at Wapping and enlarged East India Docks at Blackwall.

I have referred to ship-building in London river as early as the reign of Alfred the Great. From the ninth century it expanded continuously and in Henry VIII's reign Royal Dockyards were established at Woolwich and at Deptford which became England's principal ship-building yard. The first of the line of huge luxury transatlantic liners, Isambard Kingdom Brunel's *Great Eastern*, was built at Millwall in 1858 and warships were built on Thames-side for the Royal Navy as late as 1912.

And still expansion continued: the Millwall Dock was opened in 1869; the Royal Albert Docks in 1880, nearly two miles long and with 16,500 feet of deep-water quays; and the Tilbury Dock in 1886, carrying the length of docks and yards and warehouses of the port of London to a point twenty-six miles down river from the Pool.

Trade into and out of London river transformed hundreds of square miles of the face of England from marsh, meadow and woodland into great complexes of masonry up and down river from London, forced the river between firm banks, eliminated the marshes, speeded the current and so poisoned the water that one of the greatest salmon rivers in Europe became lifeless. A very similar transformation occurred at a different pace and on a smaller scale along the shores of Southampton Water; along the banks of the Severn estuary from Bristol; along the banks of the Tyne from Newcastle; along the Bristol Channel coast up and down from Cardiff; along the banks of the Mersey from Liverpool, covering the great mere from which the city derives its name, along the banks of Clyde and Forth and Belfast lough. On a lesser scale much the same thing happened at Middlesbrough, Hull and scores of smaller ports. At Plymouth, Portsmouth and Chatham, this transformation of country into mercantile landscape was hastened by the building of Royal Naval docks, yards and barracks. And where a port lay near to a great manufacturing area, Liverpool to Manchester for example, the intervening country was steadily eaten up as the two complexes of trade and industry grew towards each other.

By one of the ironies of economic history, the railway network began to grow all over Britain at the very moment when improved road-making and coach-building had together brought stage-coaching and the carriage of freight by road to their highest point of effieiency. As I have said, the proprietors of stage-coach lines did all in their power to hamper railway development including the cutting of fares to rates below the figure charged by the railway companies. But they were fighting a losing battle; industry, now dominating the country, required a much faster pace of living than the older way of life had done, and the important thing became speed in the carriage of passengers, freight and mail. Stage-coaching and wagon-carrying began to decline and the road network lost its importance, or some of it, and did not regain it until the perfecting of the internal combustion engine. This does not mean, of course, that the roads were quite neglected; they were still vital as feeders for the railways and for local cross-country travelling and carrying.

They might have been saved and developed into an even more complex network by a mechanical development which was never given its chance but which, just conceivably, could have aborted railway development altogether: the steam-coach. It is worth glancing briefly at this half-forgotten invention which might have given us some kind of motorways over a century ago.

The first steam-driven carriage was built and demonstrated by a French engineer in Paris in 1769; it was not a success but it did suggest possibilities. Murdoch, Boulton and Watt's brilliant foreman, invented a steam-car and built a model which worked, but Watt, who did not believe in the practicability of steam-driven vehicles and was afraid of accidents with high-pressure boilers, prevented its development. Trevithick built a steam-carriage which worked in 1801, but it broke down repeatedly, chiefly because there was as yet no metal hard and strong enough to make durable small, light, moving parts. There were several other experimental steam carriages before, in the 1820s, Gurney built steam-coaches, the body being just like that of a horse-drawn stage-coach, and using coke as fuel. So steam-driven road vehicles and the railways started neck-and-neck, and it is just conceivable that, had the social and financial opposition to steam on the roads not been so powerful, the face of Britain would never have been overlaid by the rail network.

182

Walter Hancock built successful steam-carriages in the 1830s and they were operated in regular services on the roads. His *The Enterprise* carried fourteen people, all inside, and their luggage, at speeds up to 20 m.p.h. Hancock ran it himself for several weeks of trial, between Paddington and the City, the fare being 1s. But the operating company which was to take over from Hancock and had more steam-coaches on order with him, wriggled out of their contract in the belief that they could themselves build coaches to his specification, more cheaply. They made a mess of this and the project came to nothing, but this setback did not prevent Hancock from building more and better steam-coaches which were used on regular services, carrying some thousands of passengers and completing some thousands of miles without mishap.

In 1831 Sir Charles Dance used a steam-carriage built by Gurney to run a service from Gloucester to Cheltenham: here is a *Worcester Herald* report on the undertaking:

The steam-carriage commenced running between Cheltenham and Gloucester on Monday last and has since continued to perform the journey regularly, starting punctually from Commissioner's Yard, Cheltenham at 10 and 2 o'clock, and leaving the Spread Eagle, Gloucester at 12 and 4. The carriage contains altogether twelve persons and has been filled with passengers, including a great many ladies. All the passengers who travel by it seem much pleased and agree that the motion is remarkably smooth, regular and agreeable. It runs the distance in about fifty minutes, and we are happy to add that no accident has occurred of any description.

So the thing could be done; implicit in the venture was the possibility of an enormously increased importance for the road network, and of no railways whatever, for there can be no doubt that technical difficulties would have been overcome and machinery continuously improved, although most of the other services started were bedevilled by repeated breakdowns and accidents. What prevented development was opposition from the stage-coach proprietors, whose drivers went to the length of deliberately wrecking steam-coaches by driving hard against them; and of the turnpike trustees, frightened that steam coaches would scare away the horse traffic and damage the roads. (Telford maintained that they did less damage than stage coaches.) These people also went to great lengths in their hostility to the new invention, such as having large loose stones scattered over the road surface to damage the machinery, and above all by levying penal tolls on mechanically propelled vehicles. Thus, on the Ashburton–Totnes turnpike in Devon, whereas four-horse coaches were charged 3s., steam-coaches were charged 40s.

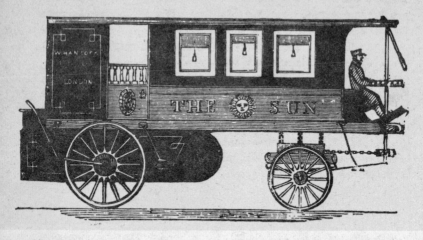

Above: *Hancock's steam omnibus, the Sun.* Below: *Horse-drawn trams drew passengers through the streets of Croydon until the steam omnibuses and then electric trams came to drive them out of existence.*

Perhaps the steam-coaches would have fought their way through and checked railway development, for not all turnpike trusts were hostile. What finally killed the mechanically propelled road vehicle was legislation obtained by the horse and coach lobby. Not only was the size and weight of the steam-coach regulated by law, but in 1865 a ridiculous Act of Parliament required that each vehicle have no less than three qualified drivers, and limited their speed to 4 m.p.h., each steamer to be preceded by a man on foot carrying a red flag.

What caused the elaboration of the road-network to be resumed and the laying down of thousands of miles of new road, sterilizing millions of acres of fertile land and covering more and more of England's face first with macadam and later with concrete, was the perfection, in about 1885, by Butler, Benz and Daimler, of a light internal combustion engine. By 1894 there were motor-cars on Britain's roads, though the 1865 law was still in force and they were supposed to be limited to 4 m.p.h. and to be preceded by that man with his red flag. But opinion had changed and that law had to go, foreshadowing the way in which laws, amenities, ways of life have fallen before the all-conquering automobile.

Three things made motoring possible, with all its consequence, so excellent in many respects, but so terrible for the look of Britain. Tar-spraying of roads solved the problem of dust; the earliest cars travelled in dense clouds of dust and heavy motor traffic would have been impossible in such conditions. The pneumatic rubber tyre was improved by the Irish inventor Doctor Dunlop. And Henry Ford's invention of the mass-produced method of manufacture made the cheap motor-car possible. The first T-model Ford came off the assembly line in 1909 and very soon thereafter began the new and ugly scarring of the land's face which this portentous event made certain.

Yet one more transport agency has, in the last decades, sterilized yet more of our fertile land, added its increment of poison to the air and yet another industrial scar to Britain's now raddled face: aviation. The first powered flight was made in 1905. Today the colossal airports required by huge jet planes and by the explosive growth of the tourist industry and mail traffic between the continents, are increasingly numerous features in the nearest open, flat country round every large city.

10 Townscape and Farmscape

A chief consequence for Britain's face of swift population growth and the agricultural and industrial expansion sketched in the foregoing chapters, was growth of towns by the addition of hundreds of miles of small- and medium-sized houses for the working and middle classes; of hundreds more churches; of all kinds of public buildings; and of great houses for the rich and mighty.

As you drive into a town of the kind whose growth has never ceased – there are many whose growth ceased for one reason or another at a particular epoch – you drive through a series of broad rings each representing one of the periods of growth, expressed in the buildings which that growth entailed. The first ring whose circumference you cross is that of the modern industrial and housing estates. Within it is the ring of streets of houses built between the two world wars, usually by speculative builders. Then comes the Victorian ring with perhaps a mere rim representing Edwardian building. Then there will be a Georgian and Regency ring, or a few streets representing those periods perhaps on one side of the town only. Finally, at the heart, is the ancient town, if anything is left of it, with, maybe, a few buildings going back to the fifteenth century and very rarely one or two even older. There may be some really rare and precious antiquity – a late Saxon or early Norman church; a castle begun in the eleventh century; and even, something still of Roman building, relics of a bath or a temple, or at least some Roman building materials built into a church or castle wall.

The scheme is not, of course, as clear-cut as that would suggest; at one period the town will have grown northward, so that when southward growth continued after a long pause, a whole epoch would be missing on that side of the town; the rings interpenetrate, are not distinct from one another; or the town may have grown longitudinally instead of expanding all round equally or even unequally.

A factor which had a very important influence on the look of Britain from the fairly early nineteenth century onwards, from the time when population growth began its fearsome acceleration, was the idealization and stylization of cottage architecture. What had originally come into existence as an expression of moderate convenience strictly controlled by economy, and which owed its appearance to the nature of the materials which could be obtained and afforded, was deliberately copied, with witty, pretty or whimsical changes, by architects designing free-standing houses, model villages or even urban terraces. Exaggeration or play upon detail produced the romantic 'old English cottage' look which became and has remained a cliché. At the same time, scores of miles of strictly utilitarian urban terraces were built, of very small houses for working people. Probably the most suitable style ever designed for this purpose was the late Georgian and Regency and very early Victorian; proportions, relation of window and door sizes and shapes to the whole terrace, and the disposition of windows were wholly pleasing because they had been more or less standardized after being abstracted from rules established in the building of the great houses of the neo-Classical kind. They were, in fact, a product of the eighteenth-century preoccupation with 'taste' and seemliness. Unhappily, the period of greatest population expansion came too late to take full advantage of this style of cottage building, and the interminable terraces of workmen's houses in such places as Merthyr Tydfil or round the later London docks were built in a debased romantic style much less suitable and much less easy to restore to seemliness after degeneration into slum.

Also out of the 'old English cottage' developed a type of middle-class house originally known as the *cottage orné*. They were irregular, low, with steeply pitched roofs and deep overhanging eaves, the walls either roughcast plaster or rubble stonework. Unlike the workers' cottages, they usually had large windows; they were decorated with much ornamental woodwork; and such climbing or clambering plants as roses, wisteria, ivy or 'Virginia' creeper were set to clamber over and embower them. In the grander examples there might also be a conservatory for exotic plants, to be used as an occasional sitting-room.

This kind of house is important because, although only a few were built as country seats for prosperous burgesses who also had a town house, they were the model for enormously more numerous derivatives. Simplified, all that careful artificial rusticity lost, its proportions degraded, it became the cliché for mile upon mile of Victorian suburban streets. So it had a powerful influence on the new look of nineteenth-century towns.

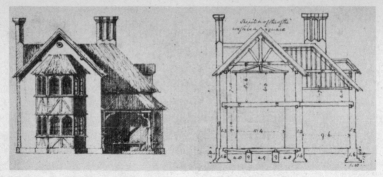

A sketch-book drawing by G. Repton of a cottage orné *inn to be built in Cheshire, showing both the elevation and section.*

Up to and for the most part including the Regency, the rule in the cases of houses built by architects, and by speculative builders applying the rules architects had agreed upon, was, in a single word, regularity. In Palladian, neo-Classical or Grecian, in revived Tudor Gothic, in all but the very new villa Italianate, a house had to be symmetrical, to fit neatly into a rectangle having certain proportions, so that the left half of the façade was a mirror image of the right. This rule was now abandoned; disregarding such classical geometry, architects allowed themselves the indulgence of designing freehand. Gables and turrets sprouted all over hugely inflated *cottages ornés*. At about the same time, English architects discovered the Tuscan villa and the Swiss chalet, and began to build here in anglicized versions of those styles.

Following a period during which one school of architects fought to retain the Grecian rule of regularity, while another was determined to restore Tudor Gothic and even an earlier and freer Gothic, because it looked, and was historically more nearly native, Gothic triumphed. The architect James Wyatt (1747–1813) was influential in this restoration of Gothic manners to English building; and it has already been noted that the Reptons, father and sons, favoured it although without departing from classical regularity. The abundant new building at Cambridge University in the first half of the nineteenth century was for the most part neo-Tudor Gothic.

The change can be noticed in the life work of more than one architect, but especially, again at Cambridge, in that of one man: William Wilkins (1778–1839). In 1806 he built Downing College in the neo-Grecian style; but by the 1820s when he was building at Trinity, Corpus Christi

Above: *the gateway of St John's College, Cambridge, built by Wilkins in a neo-Tudor style.* Below: *the facade of the British Museum in the neo-Grecian style.*

The Classical facade of the National Gallery in London.

and King's, he was wholeheartedly neo-Tudor; and the same style dominated new building at St. John's and Peterhouse. Moreover, this neo-Tudor was chosen for the building of such new public schools as Rugby.

During the last decades of the eighteenth century and the first decades of the nineteenth, neo-Grecian architecture in one of its manifestations still held its own: all Edinburgh new town was built to James Craig's plan between 1770 and 1810; the British Museum was built in 1823; St George's Hospital and University College, London, in 1827. Manchester's Royal Institute building went up in 1824; the National Gallery in 1832. Scores of industrial and country towns acquired, in the same period, their own examples of a style which the French historian of European painting and English literature, Hippolyte Taine, thought ridiculous in an English context. Perhaps he would have felt the same about the Italianate fashion which succeeded the Grecian for many purposes. He believed, what more and more Englishmen were coming to believe at the time, that Gothic building alone was native to and congruous with the English scene.

A striking detail in the look of suburban England – and it was the growth of suburbs which was the greatest transformer of England's face in the nineteenth century – is the small private garden, front and back. Contrary to popular belief it does not derive from the country or village

Semi-detached Victorian houses, built about the turn of the century in Wimbledon.

cottage garden. It is true that from Saxon times some of the English rural poor had some sort of garden; it was for the growing of vegetables and a patch of corn, and in many cases it was less a garden than a reduced smallholding. Four acres of land were in some places and at some times given to cottagers in compensation for loss of common rights. But the small garden as we know it, even the countryman's cottage garden, is of urban origin, for salad and flower gardens attached to the town houses of petty and great burgesses have a very ancient history of their own. Their story probably begins in some of the ancient free cities of Germany, Augsburg being a good example: but in both London and Paris, quite early in the Middle Ages, many burgesses had city gardens.

In the early nineteenth century one man alone had an enormous influence in setting standards of shape, lay-out and planting of the workers' urban cottage gardens, the small gardens of the new suburbs and of the larger suburban villa gardens. He was even the originator of such practices as bedding-out with plants bought from nurseries and the planting of very hardy front-garden shrubs. His name was John Claudius Loudon (1783–1843).[1]

---

[1] Some account of the life and work of this remarkable Scot will be found in my *English Cottage Gardens* (London, 1970) and my *History of Gardens and Gardening*. London, 1971.

Loudon made his name and fortune by teaching young English farmers to farm as well and as scientifically as the best lowland Scottish farmers, who, from being among the most backward in Europe, had become some of the most advanced and successful. But he was also an expert on gardening and he became a very considerable architect, especially of suburban houses. He founded magazines and edited them, wrote books and encyclopedias, and in 1838 he published *The Suburban Gardener and Villa Companion*, a book which remained influential for the best part of half a century. In it he published designs and descriptions of a great many small gardens, and explained how to plant and maintain them. He begins with the tiny gardens of workers' terrace cottages, works though the class of 'semi-detached' and small detached, up to the big suburban villa gardens which might be of many acres.

Loudon was at heart a follower of Humphry Repton; but nothing Repton had ever done, except perhaps in the making of his own private cottage garden, had much bearing on Loudon's principal work of producing standard designs for small, rectangular suburban gardens. He was at least partly and unwittingly responsible for the English fault of putting garden design well below love of flowers, for in his so-called 'gardenesque' style he conceives of good gardening as the proper display of good plants, and not as the creation of a supplementary living-room out of doors.

It was now that mile upon mile of small suburban houses acquired the small green lawns, yellow gravel, paths and beds of flowers, with some evergreen shrubs, such as spotted laurels and privet hedges which, until our own time, became characteristic of suburban scenery.

The greater garden scenery of the country was enriched and diversified by plant introduction from overseas on a scale never undertaken before, or, for that matter, since. Collectors sent home thousands of species from all over the world. The Monkey Puzzle tree, so common and incongruous in thousands of Victorian gardens, reached Britain from Brazil. David Douglas the explorer sent home maples and musk, clarkia, mahonia, flowering currant, the Douglas fir, the Monterey pine, the Sitka spruce, the Western Red cedar, the Lawson cypress and scores more. Larger and more numerous patches of Britain's face remained green all winter with the introduction by Douglas and others of hundreds of species of conifers. From China came garden chrysanthemums, camellia, peony and azalea to be added permanently to the scene. Orchids from tropical America and Asia filled the conservatories of the rich who spent fortunes on them. Barberries and escalonias from Chile began to flourish in thousands of gardens. Lilacs from France and Belgium, larches and azaleas from Japan, literally hundreds of species of rhododendrons from the Himalayas, China and North America added their evergreen foliage and spectacular flowers to English, Scottish, Welsh and Irish gardens. In south-west England, on the Welsh coast, in west and south-west Scotland and in Ulster, thousands of acres were planted with flowering trees and shrubs from Tasmania and New Zealand, from the Himalayas and the Andes, from China and Japan. Jasmines, weigelas, ornamental fruit trees, forsythias and many more plants now familiar were seen here for the first time.

It is difficult to visualize the difference made to Britain's face by the nineteenth-century plant introductions. Using the movie camera on a satellite again, the most obvious change by comparison with all earlier epochs would have been the spread of evergreens; it has continued ever since: the growing of soft woods as a crop by the Forestry Commission and by private land-owners has made certain parts of England and Wales look, from the air, as they have not looked since the pine forests spread across the land in pursuit of the retreating ice of the last glacial epoch.

A very great number of new churches were added to Britain's face at this time, built first in a manner which was a remote and debased survival of the last great phase of Gothic, later in a style which revived Gothic at its best. The difference between *survival* and *revival* in this context, is that whereas Gothic survival churches were done in a hotchpotch of Gothic manners, revival churches were usually the result of a careful study of pure styles and a reproduction of just one of them. Early in Victoria's reign it seems that the peoples of Britain began to feel about neo-Classical building much as Hippolyte Taine was to feel when he studied the face of England later in the reign.

An almost symbolic expression of this revulsion from classical rules in secular building was the Houses of Parliament (1835). This curious hybrid has the carefully measured proportions of classical architecture under a skin of Gothic ornament. The architect of the building's carcass was Sir Charles Barry, a great exponent of the Tuscan villa and other Italianate manners. The architect of the ornament, external and internal, was that great builder of beautiful Gothic churches, Augustus Pugin.

In urban, suburban and even country architecture, cement and red brick began to replace stone and white brick. And since Gothic was

Above: *the railway station at Carlisle in the Gothic style.* Below: *the Houses of Parliament by Sir Charles Barry.*

difficult for small houses, in streets or terraces, a sort of neo-Italian, debased to the point of being without grace or distinction, although remotely derived from the graceful works of men like Barry, persisted alongside an equally debased version of the 'old English cottage' and of the miniature *cottage orné*.

A new kind of public building became necessary in the second quarter of the century: the railway station; and soon hundreds of them added a new rash to the land's face. Some of the stations were noble buildings; that this was, indeed, a moment of architectural transition from classical rules to Gothic freedom can be demonstrated by looking at railway stations alone. Whereas, for example, the stations built at Birmingham and at Euston Square in 1838 were so 'classical' that they were given great entrance porches or arches serving no practical purpose, the stations for Carlisle and Perth built ten years later, were ultra-Gothic; and the Cambridge, Newcastle and King's Cross stations (1852) were neo-Roman.

But the influence of Pugin, who believed with all his heart that if only you restored medieval church architecture to England in sufficient quantity, you would restore medieval piety as well, steadily increased, through both his works and his book, *True Principles of Christian Architecture*. He built few secular public buildings or private houses – Scarisbrook Hall, Lancashire, is a good example; but his churches and those of his disciples made an impression on the look of the new suburbs all over Britain, whose face grew bristly with steeples and spires and towers as never before, almost as if we were trying to replace the destroyed forests with a forest of masonry. One single architect, Sir Gilbert Scott, alone built or rebuilt 500 churches, thirty-nine cathedrals and minsters, and twenty-five university and school buildings.

Hotel building followed railway station building at an increasing pace. As a rule, a sort of French or Italianate anti-style dominated their appearance at first; Gothic extravaganzas came later. The largest had a certain ponderous magnificence: the Grosvenor House Hotel, London, designed by James Knowles, is a fair example. Architects of these and other large buildings, including town mansions for the very rich, began to use mannerisms taken from styles from all over the world. Yet results were by no means always displeasing.

The St Pancras Station in London, by Sir Gilbert Scott, deserves a special mention, if only for one reason: had it not been for the firm intervention of Lord Palmerston, most of Whitehall would have looked like it. Scott was, indeed, the architect of Whitehall but he had to

Above: *the neo-Roman central railway station at Newcastle-upon-Tyne, Northumberland.*
Below: *St Pancras Station, London.*

sacrifice his taste to his pride in doing so important a work, under Palmerston's decree, to do it Italianate and not Gothic.

It would take volumes to describe in detail the way in which, during the bustle of architectural activity in the nineteenth century, with hundreds of thousands of houses, thousands of factories, churches, warehouses, hotels and railway stations going up all over the land, and more and more of green England going under masonry, the face of England changed. There was the widespread rash of gables and spires and Gothic ornaments; forests of chimneys grew where forests of oak had flourished; a pall of smoke covered it as once a green canopy had done; there was a new stubble of telegraph poles and the first beginnings of the wirescape netted it lightly.

There were curious colour changes: a revival, in the third quarter of the century, in the use of *terra cotta* beginning with the Albert Hall, and the Royal College of Science, introduced a lively red into the scene, as did the increasing use of red brick, while the yellow brick of London dyed miles of streets a dirty primrose. Red-brick Board Schools, the architectural expression of the 1870 Education Act, sprang up all over Britain, many of them in a kind of simplified 'Queen Anne' style favoured and popularized by the architect Norman Shaw. The return of sash windows instead of casements was one small herald of the decline in Gothicism. Chimneys on houses grew taller, gables developed sensual curves, brick and *terra cotta* ornaments broke out in strange places all over new houses.

Not only was all Britain covered then with new forms and artefacts enormously more numerous than ever before, but her facial texture was changed both by the looks of masonry and in the countryside where, too, things began to look different.

The term 'High Farming' applied to English agriculture in the second half of the nineteenth century means the application of scientific principles to agriculture. The term was coined by James Caird who, in 1850–51, toured all the agricultural districts of Britain and revealed that in a great many of them hardly any progress had been made for a century and that about one half of rural Britain was still farmed by primitive methods. On the other hand, most of the land was enclosed; there were great land-owning farmers and tenant farmers practising very modern methods of farming; and a large number of smallholdings had been replaced by a smaller number of big 'capitalistic' farms.

In 1846 the repeal of the Corn Laws removed protection from our grain-farmers and left them exposed to foreign competition. But the real effect of this measure to reduce the price of bread was long delayed. American and other foreign farmers and dealers needed time to react to the opportunity of this new market.

About seventy per cent of the land was in smallholdings: only in the south-east and south midlands were farms exceeding 100 acres in the majority. But that is in terms of numbers; a different picture emerges when we see that some 2,000 farmers held well over two million acres between them, in England and Wales, the other two million plus being divided in farms of under fifty acres. Once again, the agricultural scene was a patchwork, but of a texture very different from the patchwork of the common field. At all events, it was on the very numerous small-holdings that farming methods remained primitive, the scene much what it had been for a century: the farmers whose acreage exceeded 700 were the first practitioners of high farming.

The farming landscape varied, reflecting, in its aspect, the social history of the region. Where the enclosures were of ancient date banks were high, roads sunken, hedges overgrown into coppice, the disposition and scatter of farmhouses and farm buildings irregular. Where enclosure was modern, whether of old common land or land newly brought under the plough, as was the case on the Lincolnshire and Yorkshire wolds, farms were large, fields and buildings were laid out with method and farmsteads often quite isolated from the older villages. In the backward county of Cambridgeshire, open fields were still being worked in at least six parishes as late as 1850, and enclosure was only completed, in the parish of Hildersham, in 1889. There has, of late, been much breast-beating and cries of woe at the removal of 'ancient' hedges in the east midlands, and the creation of vast, open prairie-type fields to make large-scale mechanized farming easier: but in considerable areas of that part of England hedges are barely a century old, and the land there was farmed for 1,500 years and perhaps more in very large and hedgeless open fields.

In East Anglia, fenland left untouched by the land-drainage schemes of the past was being brought into cultivation. Steam-pumps could now be used to help dry out the land, and great modern farms were established. A similar attack on wilderness was being made at the same time in the west where, for example, farms were being made out of heath and moorland on Exmoor. And in a third manner farmlands were being extended in country which lay geographically and economically between these two extremes: at Wychwood, near Oxford, much land was not

Above: *Scarisbrook Hall, in Lancashire, in the red-brick Gothic style.*

Below: *houses in the Bedford Estate designed by Norman Shaw (see page 201).*

finally disafforested by the Crown (i.e. released from Forest Law) until 1855; but then, at last, it could be ploughed and planted.

The detail of the pattern of English agriculture also differed from region to region. On the light soils it was governed by the Norfolk four-course rotation which had been worked out and established as the best by men like Coke and Townsend in the last age of agricultural advance: this was an alternation of grain crops and fodder crops. But it had been found that, if clover and turnips were too often repeated on the same site, diseases developed, so the system was now modified by the introduction of new crops: potatoes, beans, peas, tares, kale and long-term rye-grass pastures. On the heavy soils the pattern might be quite different; the wheat-growing clays had been transformed into readily worked land by tile-drains.

Varieties of all farm crops were very much more numerous than ever before. In part this was due to the introduction of improved strains; in part to the emergence by local preferences and selection of many par-ochial strains from what had been a single widely planted variety. There were scores of locally different white and red wheats and, going only by nomenclature, about 150 varieties of potato, although very many must have been synonymous. There were some forty varieties of oats. The potato, by the way, a newcomer to England in the sixteenth century, took more than two centuries to become accepted as a field crop in all but Lancashire and parts of Wales.

Now the land was littered with farm machines never seen before: subsoil ploughs as well as ordinary ploughs; the first steam-engines for winching ploughs across big fields and back; new and improved harrows and scarifiers, drills, rakes and rollers, mole-ploughs, threshers and win-nowers, seed-dressers, feed-mills and turnip-cutters. At the head of the movement to 'industrialize' farming was the great firm of Ransome, advertising such advanced devices as combined seed and fertilizer drills which placed fertilizer several inches deeper in the soil than the seed and a foot in front of it, to give the soil time to cover the fertilizer before the seed was dropped.

But alongside all this one could still see the flail in use for threshing, the scythe for harvesting. And alongside that primitive scene, there was the really advanced scientific farm where the threshing was done by steam machinery, and a Carmichael (1820) or McCormick (1851) mechanical harvester was in use.

Livestock, again, had a new aspect. Bakewell's famous Leicester sheep had been modified in shape and improved to give those attributes required locally, by crossing to eliminate its worst faults. There was much variety, from region to region, in the look of the beef and milk cattle, from the Kyloe and Galloway herds in Norfolk and Suffolk, to the Devons and Herefords and Welsh Blacks of the midlands, and the beef Shorthorns of the northern counties. New breeds of pigs emerged and were handsomely housed in new designs of sty.

Of the living creatures of the countryside, only the people were neglected. The labourer's cottage was occasionally a pretty, always a disgraceful, feature of the landscape except where an enlightened, liberal landlord had rehoused his people in modern, model cottages. *Punch* had a famous cartoon showing Mr Punch and a rich farmer leaning over the wall of a magnificent new sty full of pampered swine, with Mr Punch saying something like, 'Fine. When are you going to do as much for your labourers?' The worker's cottage was usually a hovel with one room downstairs, one up and a lean-to shack by way of kitchen; no water or sanitation, of course. There might be two bedrooms in a few parishes. Wages were kept at starvation level, and with very rare exceptions the workers of the land got no benefit from this great period of high farming.

By about 1875, when the age of rich farming and rich farmers ended as the first huge cargoes of American wheat were unloaded in Liverpool and Cardiff, a pattern of fields and farmsteads had been laid down on most of Britain's face which lasted more or less unchanged, although slowly declining in neatness and bustle, until the First World War.

Although the ordinary manual workers were, as a rule, no better housed than the wretched farm labourers, and much worse off in that, huddled in dismal terraces for mile after dreary mile, their streets were turning into the foul slums which we have been trying to get rid of ever since, a pattern for future change which might spread downwards from the prosperous middle class, and which showed what an urban residential quarter might be like, was established by a housing experiment in the 1870s. At the time it was of interest only to the small minority of people, for not until the workers had grown strong enough, through their unions, to force the ruling classes to concede decent living standards for the miserably poor majority, could such refinements become possible for the workers and so bring about another change on Britain's face.

The architect responsible for this experiment was Norman Shaw (not related to Richard Norman Shaw), and the housing estate in question was Bedford Park, a London suburb. Shaw was, indeed, responsible for

The Dutch urban influence in the architecture of Pont Street in London.

improving much of London's face by new streets in various quarters, including Chelsea. In Bedford Park, planned as a community and at first lived in chiefly by artists and writers, he built attractive, well-designed houses in a sort of modified 'Queen Anne' style, with appropriate church and other public buildings, relatively large gardens to every house, and all the streets planted with avenues of forest trees, not the tiresome little garden trees used for street planting in later artistic suburbs.

Elsewhere in London, Manchester, Birmingham, Cardiff, Glasgow and Belfast, seemly new residential estates were engrossing more and more of the land's green face. In London, the architect Ernest George gave some Kensington streets a look of the best Dutch domestic architecture, and in scores of British towns builders, inspired by what men like Shaw and George were doing, at last found a new manner for houses which owed much to thoughtful planning for both handsome looks and interior convenience.

Later in the century towns began, as it were, to blush expansively as the use of red brick became increasingly common. The architects

... agreed style was a renaissance of the Renaissance, a Gothic game played with neo-Classical counters ... In common with all uninhibited artists they had no distaste for elaboration, and their chosen style, the wealth of their age, and the ductility of the materials nearest to their hand, bricks and terra-cotta, made elaboration easy to obtain ...[2]

The rings of suburbs round every great city went on growing. Idealized and stylized and elaborated Tudor manor-houses abounded, cottages proliferated, all very fanciful, all expressions of the vigorous confidence of the age. Using elements of antique styles was one thing; faking the antique, sentimentally reproducing even what had always been bad, even to the extent of bogus weathering, quite another. This poor-spirited mood remained unbroken up to the First World War: Sir Edwin Lutyens (1869–1944) began to restore honesty and a high spirit to the building of houses; what he started did not, indeed, have the consequences it should have had, because social pressures after the war were such that the worst kind of speculative jerry-builder was given a free hand to disfigure more hundreds of thousands of Britain's acres.

[2] H. S. Goodhart-Rendel, 1953.

11 The Advent of the Car and Electricity

Perhaps I have given an impression that the towns which, in the nineteenth century, spread out from small centres across the face of Britain were free to grow as their developers pleased. If so, it is time to correct that impression. We are used to the idea of towns growing only within the limits of regulations made by the authorities so that it is law, if anything, which controls the proliferation of today's building. Before our time there were other forces at work, forces which imparted a certain shape, or set limits to the size of a city.

We talk, rather complacently, about towns being 'organic' growths, their picturesque quality a product of our character's whimsical nature. It is true enough that to the early and middle-period capitalist, planning was anathema because, by limiting his freedom to exploit, it was thought to contravene some kind of economic law. And yet there is plenty of evidence that, where physical limitations were not placed on the developer and speculative builder, town-planning was favoured even without any intervention by the authorities. After all, the great Regency development of the Regent's Park area of London was done to a grand plan conceived by Humphry Repton and drawn by John Nash, and James Craig's Edinburgh new town, encouraged but not controlled by the municipal authorities, is another case in point. But in eighteenth- and nineteenth-century Britain the proper planning of a town was possible only where the developer could get absolute control over the whole site where his new town, or his extension of an old town, was to be built.

There are cases where this happened, and where planners were as capable of seeing the advantages of rectangular lay-outs and broad streets as any others. There is, by way of example, the case of Middlesbrough[1] where, in 1829, a partnership of Quaker capitalists, later known as the Middlesbrough Owners, bought a 500-acre site on

[1] See W. G. Hoskins, *The Making of the English Landscape*. 1955.

Nash cottages built in a ring around Regent's Park.

Teesside to build a new town. It was built on the grid plan, with every street a straight line and every corner a right-angle. And as there were then no social or economic obstacles to expansion, Middlesbrough grew with the prosperity of its industries and of its port and trade, and that gridiron rectangularity was adhered to until the later epochs of the town's history when the outer suburbs were being developed.

This was not universal because, at least in a number of important cases, the old open, common field system of agriculture had one final and in some respects disastrous effect on the look of the land's face by limiting the free spread of towns across the countryside, and so, incidentally, helping to create future slums. Where, for example, there were still common rights (e.g. the so-called Lammas grazing rights) in open fields all round an old town trying to grow, there was a serious difficulty. As we have seen, such common rights lasted, in quite a number of places, well into the nineteenth century; and where commoners refused to give up those rights for any consideration, as happened in the case of Nottingham, it was impossible for the town to grow outwards, much less according to a rational plan.[2]

[2] J. D. Chambers, *A Century of Nottingham History*. Nottingham, 1952.

But since industrial growth imposed growth on the city's population, room had to be found for people and the town had to grow. As a consequence, developers bought up every inch of open space, gardens, orchards, even courtyards. Our example is still Nottingham, which, before the building boom we are describing, was considered the most beautiful town in England, a 'Paradise regained' as it was once described by an eminent visitor. And all those open spaces were built on. There was no room for new streets, so alleys had to do instead, and wretched little houses were simply crammed in at a scandalously high density.

Thus the pig-headed last-ditch opponents of enclosure, who feared to see their lovely town cut off from the country by ring after ring of new town development, were the unwitting creators of some of the most atrocious slums in the country, a hideous blemish on Britain's face. Horrible mean terraces of back-to-back cottages faced each other across an open sewer in the service alley, and there was a population of one person to every six square yards, which meant cramming dwellings of some kind for over 800 people into every acre. This represents a density of over 50,000 people to the square mile; Britain's average population density today is about 900 to the square mile. The slum-owners did well out of this, but nobody else. Nottingham is just an example of why so many of our towns looked like they did until the slum-clearance movement of the 1930s or until the Nazi *Luftwaffe* helped us with bombs to clear up the mess which was the last consequence of the ancient village two-field or three-field system.

Where enclosure and dispossession of the commoners had come before the nineteenth-century spurt in industrial evolution and the associated population explosion, so that there was land round the town which could be bought, as in the case of Leicester,[3] then some measure of planning was possible, streets could at least be streets and not mere lanes, and conditions for the growth of the worst kinds of slums were never created.

The people who clung to their common rights, prevented the outward growth of towns and so forced on their fellow-townsmen that filling-in high-density development which swiftly degenerated into foul slums, at least had easily understandable and perfectly respectable reasons for their obstinacy: those rights might be all they had in the world, or, if they were more prosperous burgesses, they had the preservation of the town's rural associations in mind. In that respect, they

[3] Hoskins, *The Making of the English Landscape*. 1955.

showed more foresight than most people since the divorce of town from country in very large cities has proved to be a disaster for what we now call 'the quality of life'.

There were obstructionists of quite another kind at work who totally prevented the growth of some old towns. I am indebted to Professor W. G. Hoskins for permission to quote from *The Making of the English Landscape* the very revealing case of Stamford:

The open fields hemmed in the town along its northern side, while on the southern side Burghley Park and the farmlands of the Cecils offered not an acre for expansion. Here the open fields survived until 1872. Until that late date, the Cecils successfully opposed any move to enclose the fields, for reasons which were never fully disclosed at the time. But the main reason is clear enough. The borough of Stamford returned two members to Parliament, the franchise being restricted to householders. Since the end of the seventeenth century the Cecils, at Burghley House just outside the town, had controlled the election of both members by a combination of methods that seemed to leave no loophole for a mistake. There was, indeed, one possible loophole. Squatters on the waste of the manor, at the fringe of the open fields, erected hovels and tried to stake a claim. But the Marquess of Exeter (as the Cecils had become in 1801) pulled down these hovels instantly, and prosecuted the squatters. Why? Because every house that went up and stayed up represented a certain vote against his political nominees. With all his elaborate political machinery – his control of all the tradesmen in the town and of all the town's six advowsons, his ownership of some two hundred houses each carrying a vote, his absolute control of the Mayor, the corporation and all the corporation offices – the Marquess of Exeter could not be absolutely certain that the remaining voters would not one day oust his candidates. There were too many houses he did not own; and he could not afford to see any more built. In a town that chafed under his tyranny, every new house that went up was a vote against the Cecil interest.

For the same reason, therefore, he could not allow the open fields to be enclosed. That would have meant some twelve hundred acres freed for building, a catastrophic thought. True, he owned a good deal of this land and could stop any building on his own acres. But there was much he did not own. As lord of the manor, his consent was necessary to the procuring of any act of parliament for the enclosure of the town fields: and that consent was never forthcoming. . . . The people were passionately anxious that the railway should come their way, for it was plain enough that the great coaching trade, by which they lived, was doomed. For reasons we need not go into, Lord Exeter successfully prevented the main line from entering the town: it was taken through Peterborough instead. Stamford was killed: in the 1850s its population, which until then had been rising steadily, actually began to fall. There was no housing problem here. The open fields remained open for another generation – until the secret ballot came in 1872, but by then grass was growing in the streets of the town.

So Stamford's loss was Peterborough's gain; as we have seen, the coming of the railway there had set the town growing enormously. It is

'Over London by Rail' by Gustave Doré. The railways aided the growth of Victorian cities and the proliferation of quickly built back-to-back housing.

beside the point that today we have too many very ugly industrial towns marring, too few old 'unspoilt' towns adorning, Britain's face. We may wish that there had been more great land-owners as selfish, as indifferent to the future welfare of their townsmen, as the Cecils. But at the time that selfishness and indifference were economically disastrous: it is merely odd that, for the look of Britain's face, they turned out to be a boon in the long run. For Britain's face, more small towns would have been better than fewer but much larger ones.

So many different causes lie behind the looks of old towns, that one would need an encyclopedia to set them down. A few examples will do instead.

Certain English towns have what seem to be disproportionately enormous market-places, or enormously wide main streets which were, and

Stamford, which kept its basic rustic stone look, and is very much the pattern of an ancient English town today.

often still are, used as market-places. Such towns were in what was once either sheep country or country where the grazing of beef-cattle for the great urban markets was a major rural industry. Cattle and sheep markets on an 'industrial' scale take up a great deal of room. So very large market-places are a by-product of England's primacy as Europe's wool producer; or of the growth of the grazier's prosperity as London and one or two other cities created a huge demand for meat.

Rows of shops, now transformed as to the lower storey by modern fronts and plate-glass windows, often imply a row of market-stalls in the past.

Professor Hoskins has suggested an explanation of triangular market-places which sometimes determined the shape of the town growing round them, which might thus also be more or less triangular: he takes the example of St Albans which was founded and planned by Abbot

Wulsin in about 950. Wulsin made the market-place triangular because traders regarded the stall-sites near the Abbey walls, where the crowd of customers was apt to be thickest, as the best ones, so that fewer and fewer of them would want to set up stalls the farther away they had to be from the walls.

Very broad main streets may sometimes be a legacy of the need to turn wagons with their teams of oxen. The very small market-places of some towns are usually the result of building on the periphery of the original market-place when changes in the economy, declining market-trade or want of room for expanding the town outwards, forced the municipal authorities to license building on such sites.

Once such obstructions as common rights and aristocratic power disappeared – the latter hardly survived the First World War – there was no barrier to the expansion of towns and cities, wherever land could be bought for development. Then a new burst of urban growth occurred between the two world wars until it was checked by the financial depression of 1929.

A relatively new phenomenon which added a fresh blemish to England's face was the kind of linear urban sprawl called 'urban development'. There were two main causes of this: the first was the motor-car. Little did we realize in the flush of excitement at having a means, soon available to millions of people, of increasing our freedom of movement so enormously, that the car would force us to distort the shape of our towns and, with the motorways, our countryside, to suit it.

The swift proliferation of motor-cars in Britain called for enlargement and improvement of old roads and the building of new ones; and notably of the so-called arterial roads which, while they were certainly not motorways in our sense of the word, were the first roads to be built specifically for the motor-car. Now, as will be clear from earlier chapters in this book, transport highways invariably attract settlements. The early colonists of Britain settled beside rivers, once tree clearance was no longer an impossible problem, because rivers were their highways. The Roman roads called new towns into existence. Saxon villages on important roads grew into towns extending along those roads. As fast as canals were cut, industries moved out and established themselves along the canal banks near industrial towns, and residential districts came into existence for the factory workers. The railways, too, brought new towns into existence and caused old ones to grow much larger.

But there was a difference in the settlements attracted to arterial

A network of roads and later motorways began to grow specifically to cater for a constant stream of commuting traffic. Above: *the M1 near Hemel Hempstead.*

roads, due in part to the fact that road transport is much more flexible than any other kind; the railways stimulated the growth of towns round the railway stations: but the motor-car and the motor-bus need no stations, can stop anywhere on a road. So the new settlements could be linear, and shallow: and Britain's enormously increased population made them on such a scale that great and lasting damage was done to the face of the land.

Above: *All of England is being covered with systems of roads which come together in complex cloverleaf junctions.* Below: *main roads with shops clustering along their edges. Instead of shopping in village centres, where people could congregate, the cluster of shops is now bisected by a large road, full of fast-moving traffic, separating the two halves, at peak shopping hours.*

The second major factor which made this kind of ribbon development along roads possible was the emancipation of industry from direct reliance on coal. The use of energy derived from fossil fuels, first coal, later oil, in the form of electricity which can be conveyed to any point in the land instantaneously and continuously, meant that while industry was still indirectly dependent on coal or oil for its power-driven machinery, and homes for heating, lighting and cooking, there was now no advantage in locating industrial plant, and therefore housing estates, in coalfields: electricity was no dearer and no more difficult to get a hundred miles from the power generator than in its shadow. So, for the sake of easy transport of goods and raw materials, factories could now be sited on the new motor roads; with the factories came the housing estates, together creating shallow roadside conurbations scores of miles long. Such conurbations required certain services: more or less unsightly petrol filling stations became a roadside feature, and great ugly parking-places where truck drivers could pull off the road and get a meal at cheap restaurants, usually housed in wooden sheds. The roads called new public houses and road-houses into existence as well and, with the housing estates, roadside terraces of shops. Thus came into existence those many miles of road from which it looks as if all Britain must be built on; only a view from the air reveals the thinness of these strange long towns, and the still broad acres of open farming country behind them.

It was loudly condemned by many as ruinously unsightly, spoiling great areas of Britain's face from the aesthetic point of view; and there were regulations and even legislation to check its growth. But there may be something to be said for it. It prevents or it can be used to prevent, sprawl over large areas of the land; and, given the motor vehicle as your means of transport and freight-carrying, it is efficient, since every destination served by the vehicle is on the same road where traffic can be concentrated, thus sparing the old towns. However, planning opinion is against it because it is felt that a town should be compact and built round a centre, a place for people, not for machines, and no new town has been deliberately built in this linear form.

The universal use of electrical energy in Britain added yet another ugly blemish to its face: the wirescape. We have seen that it began with the telegraph and telephone wires and poles, but those were relatively inoffensive objects in the landscape. The full and fair distribution of energy to all consumers needed a distributive system such that the energy

Pylons, marching across the English countryside, showing the cultivation of crops under and around the towers.

generated at power stations, wherever they were located in the country, could be fed to industry and homes everywhere. The national grid was the result, and in due course all Britain was netted in a complex of huge cables carried by tall pylons striding up hills and down dales, across plains and rivers, straddling roads and even towns.

Not everyone agrees that pylons and their cables are hideous: some consider that a long line of those steel towers with their joining swags of cable adds drama and human meaning to a landscape. To most people, however, they are an eyesore: could they have been avoided? Technically, it is possible to put high-tension cable under ground; there are serious problems but they can be solved and in the future we may decide that the wirescape should not be extended and ought to be slowly eliminated.

The great housing and industrial building development stimulated by the growth of light and of electrically powered industry along the arterial roads produced by the motor-car and truck came at a bad time for architecture.

'Functionalism', first preached by an Englishman, Professor W. R. Lethaby (1857–1931), and first practised with fame by one or two German architects and by the Frenchman Le Corbusier, is the principle that a building should be rigorously designed to serve exactly the purpose it is intended for, and not primarily as an object to be looked at with enjoyment. Not that the Functionalists simply dismissed the aesthetic aspect of building as totally irrelevant or without importance: their view was that an artefact, whether a house or any other manufactured article for use is beautiful if correctly designed as the expression of its function. An example is the Concorde aeroplane: it is an expression of the function of fast, passenger-carrying flight, and designed rigorously with that function in mind: and it is certainly beautiful. A factory should be designed as a machine is designed, for doing exactly the job it is intended for. And a dwelling house should be a kind of machine designed for living in. In theory, the guiding principle of inter-war industrial and institutional building was this Functionalism. And this was all the more understandable in that the new methods of building with steel-reinforced concrete meant that designers of large buildings had to be primarily engineers rather than architects in the classical sense. It naturally took a long time to raise and train a first generation of men who were, ideally, both.

As a matter of fact, the aesthetic damage done to the land's face would have been considerably less had Lethaby's principles and Le Corbusier's practice been applied to the new factories, shops, public houses and so forth, by people who were pure engineers with no architectural pretensions. The reason why such large areas of the Britain we have inherited are ugly, is not that architects were too 'functional' in their vision, but that they were not functional enough.

As it was, unable to break with the past idea of the architect's role, architects made all kinds of very unhappy attempts to disguise the function of their buildings with ornament totally inappropriate and out of scale. Moreover, in despair because the new functions, and the scale of the works they demanded, could not be expressed in any of the old terms (you could hardly build a modern factory to look like a cathedral or a town hall, or a palace), architects shopped around in cultures alien in spirit and remote in time from our own, thus producing horrible parodies of Egyptian, Mayan and other strange manners, with aesthetically disastrous consequences.

The housing estates, although far from satisfactory, were not quite as bad as this. But their mere extent was a blemish. First they lined the

Above: *Cité Radieuse – Unité de Habitation, Marseilles, built by Le Corbusier.*

Below: *Functionalism in modern design: the Concorde in flight.*

new roads, then they filled in the rectangles and triangles between such new roads, until they composed those vast 'subtopias' which are and probably always will be an outrage on Britain's face. In design, a number of building fashions succeeded or overlapped each other, as speculative developers and builders sought 'selling points' which would recommend their products to a public with no sure aesthetic standards and a nervous taste for either novelty on the one hand, or 'safe' tradition on the other. Most of these new houses were bad fakes of old styles: scores of miles of houses were built to look half-timbered, but the timbering was sham; there were whole estates of 'old English' cottages, of base and degenerate descendants of Tuscan villas. And worst of all was the ornamented nondescript.

There were also a few housing estates or ribbon developments intended to cash in on the interest in Functionalism, and known as 'modernistic'. For a few years a minority of the British amused themselves with these products not of studied function (the truth is it turned out to be impossible to improve on a square Georgian house as a 'living-machine') – but of the salesman's and advertiser's desperate need to have something 'different' to offer.

Economic and social change made one colossal blot on Britain's face by grossly over-enlarging London and some other cities. A population drift away from the nineteenth-century regions of staple industry in the north, to the south-east and south, began soon after 1920 and has continued for half-a-century. Why? The answer is complex.

Until 1914 the older, staple industries of the north and midlands, and of the Welsh coalfields, were the sources of our principal exports, and England was still the greatest industrial power on earth. After 1918 other manufacturing countries began to overtake us very rapidly. The absolute importance of the staple industries declined to only relative importance, and new, light industries – electrical household equipment; the first man-made fibres like rayon; radio; aluminium ware; synthetic dyes; sugar from our home-grown beet – were developed in the low-rated areas of the south. More and more people moved south to man these industries, and south Wales, Lancashire and the West Riding of Yorkshire, their erstwhile quasi-monopoly gone, became 'depressed areas', that is, areas of rapidly declining industry and large-scale unemployment.

Now, a very large city with its suburbs, or a newly developed urban area based on new industries, needs an increasing supply of distributive

and service trades – shops, maintenance firms, plumbers, electricians and so forth. Technological advances in both the old, heavy industries, now forced to compete with foreign competitors, and in the new, light industries, all in the general direction of increased automation, meant that the proportion of labour used in production kept falling while the proportion engaged in the service and distributive trades rose. Workers consequently flowed in an ever increasing stream into the south-east. The process was cumulative: the larger Greater London grew, the larger it must continue to grow unless checked by deliberate interference by government. A vast area of England's face went under bricks, mortar, stone and concrete for the housing, employment and transportation of more than a quarter of Britain's entire population.

There were other, lesser shifts which affected Britain's looks: when, about 1936, a measure of rearmament was undertaken in the face of the threatening posture of the totalitarian powers – Nazi Germany, Fascist Italy and Stalinist Russia – a new consideration led to changes in some of the towns and countryside of the south-west and west. It was necessary to site new factories, especially armament factories, as far as possible out of reach of air raids from the Continent. Today, of course,

Opposite and above: *Parodies of the Mayan, Egyptian and Tudor styles.*

Above: 'modern' housing in many ways is worse than the earlier parodies, because it has no distinct style of its own.

nowhere in Britain is out of reach of missile weapons sited thousands of miles away: but in the 1930s the fantastic development of aviation technology and rocketry was simply not foreseen. Workers were thus drawn away from regions of very high unemployment, to man the new factories; and this new resettlement again attracted service trades, with another build-up of population and another outburst of new building. Architects continued to make timid use of the new engineering methods – to develop a new architecture. For example: where steel provides the bearing strength, massive piers and pillars are not necessary, they can be light and slender; but at that time architects obstinately continued to encase steel stanchions in unnecessary masonry or concrete which they were apt to cover with irrelevant ornament. In other respects, too, buildings whose appearance should have been a function of the strength of their steel framework were made to pretend that they still depended on the demands of traditional materials. Only shortly before the Second World War did some architects, influenced by French and American example, begin to exploit engineering methods of building, instead of treating them as shameful vices to be concealed by putting them into fancy dress. In the 1930s there were millions of people who hid their telephones under crinolined dolls: quite a lot of the aspect of built-on Britain owes its look to much the same spirit of archness.

Just as railways had necessarily dotted England's face with railway stations, so the invention of the moving picture spotted it with another new kind of building, the cinema. At first they had none of the solidity, or architectural pretensions of the theatre, and the earliest cinemas were built as barns or long sheds with more or less flashy façades stuck on to them.

Probably the first English cinema with architectural claims was the Regent Cinema in Brighton, which was built in 1921. What is now the Odeon in Kensington, built in 1925, was also of high quality. But it was some time before the standard set by these two was lived up to. In the late 1920s and early 1930s the look of hundreds of urban high streets was altered by the addition of super-cinemas. Most of them had the blatancy of an advertisement hoarding or the ephemeral look of a temporary building run up for an exhibition. In a few cases something worth looking at was added to the scene. But cinema design has produced some exciting cases in retrospect which belie the ideas of functionalism.

At night, electric street lighting restores the topography of our cities.

The interior of the Regent Cinema at Brighton.

A city built on a group of hills retains, of course, its 'relief'; but cities built on gentle slopes seem always to appear flattened by the load of masonry laid upon the land. You may feel the slope as you walk, but you cannot see it; or your car may surprise you by running gently forward or backward in a traffic jam on a street you had always supposed level. But stand on a roof or at a high window or on the highest hill in the city, and look over it at night, and see how the rows of street lights rise in gentle curves, dip, rise again, revealing the shape of the land it was built on, giving back to us the hills and valleys.

Nor is this all the transformation magic of electric light. The advertisement posters and hoardings of posters, another feature of cities peculiar to our times, provide nothing like such entertainment for the eye as the neon-light night-time advertisements. Their messages may be vulgar, meretricious, untrustworthy or downright fraudulent; that is not our point – *caveat emptor*, merchants have always been given the freedom to deceive. It is the medium itself which is a source of pleasure, giving our nocturnal city scene a kind of gaiety.

Then there is the new art of floodlighting, drawing every exquisite detail of our most beautiful ancient buildings, every boldness of our most striking new ones, out of the darkness, and making it seem as if the buildings themselves are luminous.

Lighting is still a young art: floodlighting is its subtlest manifestation, and one which will be developed, so that at night time, instead of being stippled with a myriad points of light like another firmament full of constellations, the face of Britain will one day glow with hundreds of cities each seeming to give out light from all its many surfaces.

12   After the Bombing

The transformation of Britain within a mere 2,000 years from a land of primeval forest, swamp and upland with a few small outposts of European civilization connected by a small network of roads, into what it looked like by the 1930s is quite startling. No less so, surely, than the transformation of that other territory which was colonized from Europe – North America.

By 1930, Britain was already grossly overcrowded with the products of man's work and the debris of human life, lined and wrinkled with roads, railroads and waterways, stippled all over with towers and chimneys, scarred with quarries, pits and mineheads, and horribly littered with the rubbish taken from underground.

In every century some part at least of man's work on Britain's face has been beautiful. But after the First World War it began to be clear to a few people who had eyes to see, that greed, haste and altogether too much respect for the 'right' of a man to do what he liked with land he had paid for, had spoilt the quality of life over vast areas of Britain by creating, in the major industrial regions and the huge conurbations, an environment so hideous and so uncomfortable to live in, that only to look at it was to be angry. Men with a certain kind of training in the sciences and arts could see, moreover, that if we had taken our raw material – the green land of the Windmill Hill people – and made it over to our purposes with forethought, instead of in a series of profit-rushes, we might have had all the wealth of industry and all the amenities of civilization, without such hideous marring of the land's face. But that is only technically true: socially and politically, the mess was inevitable; as a community we did not know what we were doing.

The industrial way of life had to be pioneered; certain accidents of character, history and geology appointed Britain to that task; industrialism could only, in the first instance, have developed in a society in which men ambitious of wealth and power were free to find new ways of exploiting skills, resources and labour. In an unfree society – for example, an Oriental tyranny on the old model – the ruling caste has no motive, the people no means, to pioneer mechanized industry. But the very fact that industry based on mechanical power could develop only in a free society, meant that development could not be planned or controlled until so much damage had been done to the environment, the quality of life and the souls and bodies of workers that measures of control and restriction became acceptable.

One of the disadvantages of being a pioneer in industrial invention and development is that when better, cleaner, handsomer ways of doing things emerge as a result of experience and of technological progress, you are left with a lot of old, obsolete machinery and buildings on your hands – steam-driven plant when the latest is electrical; coal-fired furnaces when the latest is oil; residential and industrial slums and hideous urban sprawls when in countries which came later to industrialization, and so had the benefit of your experience and mistakes, machines and people could be housed in a more seemly fashion. In theory, of course, you can clear away all the old mess, rebuild and re-equip – ultimately, you have to do so. But the old plant, old houses, old factories, ugly and inefficient though they may be, represent enormous material and intellectual investment: and it is hard to determine to scrap them, to write them off.

We have seen also, when considering the population drift to the south-east, with its consequences for England's face, what happens when old industries run down and new ones spring up. All the ugly scars – unsightly factories, hundreds of miles of mean, grim streets, coal-tips and slag heaps, dead and blackened country, foul air and polluted water – all this was half abandoned; new land was invaded, more green and pleasant places were put under masonry, and a new ugliness too often created without any attempt to clear up the old one. In a private-enterprise society it is very difficult to force the capitalist to clear up and tidy the place behind him; ultimately the community as a whole, by voting resources for the work, is obliged to do it for him.

The most recent changes in Britain's face were mostly due to the Second World War and its social, political and economic aftermath. There was wider distribution of wealth accompanying a new, fast spurt in industrial evolution which brought greater productivity. A wider acceptance was given to socialism. Even the anti-socialist attitudes and declarations of some politicians are parts of this political power game. All capitalist societies are increasingly socialist in, for example, their

National Parks preserve what remains of the 'natural' beauty of England. Above: Exmoor and the Exe valley in Somerset.

welfare contracts or legislation. Socialism now amounts to the idea that the community can and must exercise an increasing measure of control over private enterprise in order to protect itself and its environment from the consequences of the exploiter's greed.

These things all involve planning of development at both local and national levels. Building developers can no longer be allowed to build where and how they like, but have to submit to regulations, and to get the community's permission to carry out their plans. Towns are no longer allowed to go on sprawling over more and more countryside, but instead whole new towns are planned in advance. Areas of outstanding natural beauty are designated and building on them is prohibited. National parks are created to try to preserve something of Britain's older, wilder face. As well as the authorities, the National Trust plays an important part in preserving large areas of Britain from aesthetic ruin. Industry is barred from some parts of the country and attempts are made to bring some order and seemliness into its growth in others. Steps are taken to persuade or induce great industrial companies to reanimate and redevelop the older industrial regions and to clear up some of the past's mess in the process. Some effort is made to force both nationalized and private industrial undertakings to tidy up after some of their dirtier operations, such as open-cast mining. Zones are designated where it is illegal to produce dirty smoke from either industrial or domestic chimneys.

The new spirit which we owe to the pioneer conservationists and environmentalists, in which we now try to minimize the ugly mess which is too often a by-product of industry, and even to clear up the mess left by the past, is well exemplified by the joint work of the National Coal Board and the Forestry Commission in the south Wales coalfield. Those huge and hideous coal-tips are being first shaped by bulldozers working to carefully prepared profile drawings based on three-dimensional models, to match the natural contours of the Welsh hills; and then planted with one or two of the few species of trees which grow well on them. The time will come when only an expert eye will be able to distinguish the natural from this 'reconstituted' landscape.

Since the eighteenth century, philosophers have been keeping a worried eye on population growth and uttering warnings of possible disaster to come. But they were individuals thinking and working in semi-isolation and making an impression only on a few people and in the very long term. Now, for the first time, all of us are made aware of the danger to our standards and quality of life implicit in the arithmetic of

This winding road in the Isle of Wight follows the contours of the English landscape.

population growth. We begin to see that, unless we plan our ways and places for living, working and playing very carefully, Britain must become a very unpleasant place to live in. And there are other very powerful forces, deriving from the same source – industrial growth plus wider spreading of wealth – at work, hampering our efforts to preserve the humane way of life: unfortunately our society's survival depends upon industrial growth, the condition in which the working class can be given a higher and higher consumption-potential (more commonly called 'standard of living') without requiring the managerial and bureaucratic class to cut down its consumption and investment. There are, it is true, alternative societies, but at the time of this writing they seem unlikely, except in the event of one of those overwhelming catastrophes we are more or less continuously threatened with, to become acceptable to a majority of citizens. Industrial growth to which no limit is, or perhaps can be, set by an intelligent decision, must, short of the new age of extra-terrestrial exploration and colonization in which, very significantly, science-fiction novelists take refuge, lead to a dead-end, at which socialization $\times$ technology $\times$ resources can go no further: in other words, the territory, the ant-hill, the hive. In that case, of course, this book is a short history of a process with no more significance than that of the evolution of the ants. I prefer to believe that, somehow, it is not going to happen that way.

We have already said a good deal about the influence of motor vehicles on Britain's face. After the Second World War this became more pernicious, as the wider distribution of wealth and the huge growth of the credit system – hire purchase and other ways of borrowing from the future – made car-owning possible for more and more people.

The cheap, private motor-car is a great boon: it gives the ordinary human being seven-league boots; in the power of movement overland he becomes a giant; but giants, of course, take up more room than people of human size. A man in movement on his feet occupies, at any given moment of time, about four square feet of surface; but an automan – that man–motor-car creature which is more or less the typical inhabitant of a modern industrial country – at any given moment occupies something like fifty square feet.

To cope with the motor-car explosion and its growing place in our lives we are forced to modify the shape of our cities to suit not man, but automan. Some of the new towns we have built in the past quarter of a century have been deliberately designed for automan: the centre of Birmingham, and Milton Keynes, for example; and a town designed for automan cannot become a community of men, like a village or a small town. In the second place, we have had to lay down on the face of Britain, and are still doing so, a whole new network of roads especially designed for and exclusive to automan. At the time of writing, we have had about 1,000 miles of motorway forced on us by the greedy demands of the motor-car; and under them lie many thousands of acres of Britain's once green face.

The motor-car as vermin has altered the land's face in another way. One of the benefits it confers is that of enabling people to go and see beautiful places; and it would be ridiculous to blame people for doing what men of liberal education and means have always done and urged others to do. Unfortunately a beauty spot suffers once a carpark is attached to it, and when it is being trampled over by thousands of people at one time.

Nor is it only in the country that the motor-car does this kind of aesthetic damage: park motor-cars in and round a beautiful square in a great city, and the proportions of the square, which are its beauty, are changed, ruined.

Clearly, then, the motor-car has had a great direct and indirect influence on Britain's face in our time. In itself it is neither good nor bad; being only a tool, it is neutral; but it is permissive of evil. It could be that it is teaching us a bitter lesson: that freedom destroys the conditions in which freedom can exist. In that respect it is like the great industrial private enterprises of the last two hundred years. It may be, of course, that we have come to the conclusion that freedom is impossible and that the territory, the anthill, the hive, is what we have, without being aware of it, chosen; as the Arabs say – take what you want, says God; and pay for it.

The internal combustion engine applied to machines of another kind has also changed the farming face of Britain in certain parts of the country.

The modern motorized farm machines were developed in North America for the cultivation of enormous, unbroken, unenclosed expanses of land. They make possible the working of thousands of acres with very few hands. But these machines, like the multi-share ploughs and the combine harvesters which reap, thresh and bag grain in a single operation, can only work efficiently in a vast prairie and are simply unmanageable in a small, hedged field. Consequently, where they are being used in Britain, they have reversed the change which occurred when enclosures were in progress: hundreds of miles of hedges which were planted then have been grubbed up; and in some respects parts of the landscape of the east midlands and East Anglia are now nearer what they were in the seventeenth century than in the early twentieth, although the patchwork surface has not, of course, also been restored.

The Nazi air force, in 1940–41, destroyed considerable areas of a number of our cities, including London, so that even had no other forces been at work to compel us, we should have had to make good the damage in a new spurt of building which made changes on Britain's face. The look of many cities today is not the 1939 look.

Every year we add to Britain's face between 350,000 and 500,000 new dwellings, either individual houses, or as blocks of flats. Local authorities are responsible for about half this total. The most striking of these residential buildings now added to the look of the land are the tower-blocks like those of the famous Roehampton housing estate. Such towers have been condemned by critics on two grounds: that they are incongruous with the look and scale of our country, and that they are 'inhuman'. As to the first objection, it must be repeated that Britain has no changeless 'look'; its face has been changing since it emerged, raw material for the men to come, from the creative labour sketched in Chapter 1. As for the second objection, opinion polls of tenants show that at least as many people like as dislike living in hives – I mean towers.

The Roehampton towers.

There has been at least one great advance in big buildings since engineering methods of erecting them first replaced traditional building methods: harmony between engineering and architecture has been achieved, at least in the best towers. On the other hand, engineering methods do make it very difficult for architects to establish a style which could properly be identified as British. The face of Britain is perhaps destined to look less and less 'British', more and more 'European': and yet, as I have said, national stylistic differences do emerge and the Roehampton development is a case in point.

The Roehampton development is a model – only as regards looks, lack of social insight has made it far from a model in certain other respects – of what the housing estates which may cover more and more of Britain's face can look like. It mingles the work and personal styles of several architects: the Alton East Estate part, by Oliver Cox and Rosemary Stjernstedt, derives its plan from Scandinavian ideas, but surely, in scale and feeling, it is recognizably British? In the Alton West part, by Colin Lucas, John Killick and Bill Howell, the inspiration is Le Corbusier; but the treatment has a delicacy, a lightness, which French building on this scale does not attain. Compare Roehampton or the tower-blocks between Tower Bridge and Greenwich along the Jamaica Road route, or for that matter the much abused but, in fact, beautiful Centre Point tower, with the deeply depressing *cités* groups of workers' tower-dwellings round Paris. The French are good at realizing SF dreams like the Charles de Gaulle airport buildings; but bad at housing people. Only the Italians and the English have developed a vernacular tower-dwelling. It is as if the special character which distinguished English Gothic is re-emerging in English Modern.

The objection that this kind of building is 'not on the human scale' makes the mistake of regarding humanity as changeless beyond some point in its evolution which the objector has decided, to suit his own taste, is the right point to stick at. But in reality, the evolution of society is always modifying the meaning of the word 'human'. Every 'modern' man in the last several centuries has tapped a mighty increment of physical power in the form of ingeniously applied mechanical energy. Where our ancestors moved at five or ten miles an hour, we move at six or seven hundred. A man digging a ditch in the past removed a few cubic feet of soil in an hour; his descendant removes a few thousand cubic feet in the same time. The calculation which the mathematician working for the engineer once took many weeks to complete, is completed for him in a second or two by a computer: one could go on with such comparisons for an hour, but the point is surely made. Today's man looks deceptively like yesterday's, but, I repeat, he is a sort of giant, and the 'scale' of humanity is not, today, what it was yesterday.

To return to that Roehampton housing estate: it is exemplary in another aspect; the architects made extremely good use of the hilly, wooded site to make buildings and setting harmonious; their building did not mar but made a landscape, and in that respect their work is in the traditions of Capability Brown and Humphry Repton.

Not all local authorities' housing developments are, of course, of that kind: houses as well as flats are built, low blocks as well as high ones. Enormous housing estates have covered more and more of Britain's face with the nondescript and commonplace products of anti-architecture; in other places the universal style, often in a Scandinavian version, has prevailed. Private enterprise housing has, on the whole, contributed generously to the marring, and meagrely to the making, of Britain's latest face. Curiously enough an admirable late-nineteenth-century innovation, the artistic garden-suburb, has had a pernicious influence. Standardized, utterly undistinguished garden-suburbs meanly conceived and carried out have spread over large areas of open country where they are, even at their best, inappropriate and where new villages and new small towns would be, at least visually and probably socially, a much better answer. And as ribbon development along main roads has never been quite checked, nor filling-in between the developed strips, the subtopian blight is, despite controls, still spreading like a skin disease over Britain's face.

Not all private enterprise housing development has been bad, far from it. The architect Eric Lyons' 'Span Development' suburbs, in which the whole area – houses in a landscaped park, as it were – is planned as a unity, have none of the demerits of garden suburbs and, again, many of the elements derived from the very English genius of Capability Brown and Humphry Repton.

A change in Britain's urban face as it was during the first half of our century has been wrought by the rehabilitation, still progressing, of old urban and suburban zones. Streets, and ultimately whole quarters, of small Regency, early Victorian and middle Victorian houses, frequently with much architectural merit, which had sunk into the condition of semi-slums, have been restored to use and seemliness; and they have thus recovered something of an urban physiognomy: I say *a* past, and not *the* past, to emphasize once again the point that there is no immutable England, no changeless Britain.

Office buildings as well as flats have added many hundreds of new towers to Britain's face. Socially, they are often pernicious: in some cases they stand empty for years, while the process of inflation continuously increases their money value for the speculative developer who built them. But visually many are pleasing and some of them magnificent. Among the most impressive of these towers are the Millbank Tower, Centre Point, the Hilton Hotel and the Post Office Tower in London, and the towers of the splendid Tricorn Development in Portsmouth. But I must not make overmuch of towers, they are not the only striking new features with which industry has endowed the face of Britain: there are remarkable townscapes created by such complexes as Norgas House and the Gas Research Station at Killingworth near

Span-development houses at New Ash Green.

Newcastle-upon-Tyne; Mallinson's remarkable complex of timberyard in London's East End; a great deal of Coventry, including its beautiful railway station, the Princess Margaret Hospital at Swindon, and scores more.

Visually, and as a portent for the future, the changes made on Britain's face by the building of new universities are of more importance than all these others. The university architects have accomplished wonders in the high-density housing of communities as numerous as those of a large village, and by so doing have shown what a modern village could be like. They have often had eighteenth-century landscaped parks to build on, and have shown the way to making a harmony between buildings and landscape which does not entail the boring sprawl of the garden-suburb. Of course, those new town builders, who have been over-influenced by the garden-city ideas of that great urban-planning reformer Ebenezer Howard (1850–1928), had to accommodate the taste of Britain's lower middle and working classes for small, private gardens, so that other social and aesthetic considerations could not take priority.

233

New 'Towers of London'. Above left: *Centre Point.* Above right: *the Millbank Tower.* Below left: *The London Hilton, and* below right: *The Post Office Tower.*

The Tricorn Shop Centre in Portsmouth.

Essex University, about its lakes and its park at Wivenhoe, is virtually a 200-acre town planned and built for the housing, teaching and recreation of about 6,000 people. Ranges of low buildings alternate with groups of towers to create movement, contrast and a pleasing irregularity of skyline. The complex was not finished when this book was written but the completed project could be envisaged in the architects' model. The principal buildings there and at York University represent a new architecture in Britain, boldly modern yet successfully married to the landscape. Another example making use of an eighteenth-century park is the university of East Anglia where the range of buildings is bonded into a visually exciting unity by overhead walkways like a continuous bridge. In these and other cases, diversity in concept, execution and even in materials reveals our new architecture to be as rich in ideas as it is lively.

The idea that it was better to build new towns than to overcrowd and overextend old ones was first treated as a theoretical possibility by Ebenezer Howard in a book called *Garden Cities of Tomorrow*. Howard saw that there was something analogous to an organic relationship between the various parts – residential, industrial, commercial,

The library and dormitory blocks of Essex University.

recreational – of a city; and that overgrowth, whether of part or whole, so disturbed that relationship that the city could no longer function properly and ceased to be a setting and a machine for the good life. Ebenezer Howard's merit lay in restating this idea in modern terms, for it is, in fact, a very ancient one. To quote Sir Lewis Mumford:

Aristotle's conception that there is a right size for a city, big enough to encompass all its functions but not too big to interfere with them, was restated in modern times by Howard.[1]

Aristotle thought that the right population for a city was 30,000, with another 2,000 in the agricultural belt surrounding and supplying the city. Whether by coincidence of judgement or by derivation, when Leonardo da Vinci (1452–1519) planned the breaking up of sixteenth-century Milan, with its chaotically overcrowded 300,000 population, he proposed to build ten new cities of 30,000 people each to rehouse the

[1] From Sir Lewis Mumford's introduction to F. J. Osborn and A. Whittick, *The New Towns*. London, 1969.

Milanese. What a pity his plan was not adopted: we should have had ten cities town-planned and partly designed by the greatest genius of his and perhaps any other age. The point is, however, not that exact figure, but that there are upper and lower limits within which, and only within which, a city can really function as a city should. It is thought that about 15,000 is the lower limit, and about 100,000 the upper limit: there are social gains above the 15,000 mark up to about the 100,000 mark: above that figure, there are no more social gains; and above 300,000 serious social losses begin.

Whether or not Howard can be held responsible for the confusion of town-planners between the garden-city he conceived, and the garden-suburb, like Hampstead's, is a question: Sir Lewis Mumford thought that nobody could have made such a blunder. The fact remains that made it was and has consistently been, and in some of our own new towns the confusion has had unfortunate consequences. On the other hand not that confusion, but our obstinate preference for a certain kind of housing, for what I shall call soft-centred towns or inflated villages, may have been responsible for some aesthetically and socially unfortunate consequences. It is here that we touch for the first time on the principal obstacle in the way of making Britain a new face which shall be a mighty work of art. Whatever may be said in their favour, and there is certainly a great deal, Letchworth and Welwyn, the first two garden cities, have remained garden-suburbs, and seem to me never to have achieved the quality, feeling or atmosphere, of a city as one experiences it in even the smallest Italian cities, but still to be *sub*-urbs looking in vain for an *urbs*. And despite the deliberate and thoughtful creation of 'centres', the error has been repeated in the more recent new towns; to a depressing extent they are not quite cities. The point is important because in the future we are going to have to build more new towns if we are as determined as we seem to be to prevent the already overgrown ones, the 'million cities' as Sir Frederick Osborn calls them, and even those in the half-million category, from continuing their cancerous growth.

The first new town added to Britain's face after the Second World War was Stevenage, created round the nucleus of an existing small town with a population of 6,500. The new Stevenage was to have a population of 60,000 people, with an industrial zone and six neighbourhoods of about 10,000 people grouped round the old town, each neighbourhood having its own schools, shopping centre and community centres. There is a lot of open space, including the Fairlands Valley which is countryside

The market square of Stevenage new town.

inside the town; and these things are desirable. Yet – again – the wide sprawl of the town makes real civic feeling hard to develop and puts far too much emphasis on the motor-car.

It proved impossible to keep Stevenage down to 60,000 people; after the possibility of planning for 150,000 had been examined and rejected, 80,000 plus natural growth was decided on. Hence, more sprawl, with outlying parts of the town as much as two miles from the centre. Why? The insistence of a majority of people on an individual house with a garden: and that, in short, is the obstacle between us and a Britain of *urbs* and *rus*, rather than a Britain of suburbs.

The new town of Crawley, built round a small old town of that name, and two villages, total population 9,500, was the second of the post-war new towns. A population of 56,000 with eventual growth to 80,000 was allowed for. There are nine neighbourhoods and three parks, and each neighbourhood has the makings – schools, shops, etc. – of a complete community. But the London to Brighton road, carrying traffic moving at 70 m.p.h., cuts the town in two; and with an area of 6,000 acres it is doubtful whether population density is high enough for the generation of any civic spirit of the kind which would bring the town to life as a real *urbs*. Significantly, a report which was made by the development corporation reveals the *sub*-urban rather than urban 'image' of the new towns:

Flats have been erected in decreasing proportion as once tenants decide to *come into the country* to live, they almost universally prefer a house with a garden.[2]

The italic is mine; and those four italicized words pose a threat to the future of Britain's face: if people moving out of the overgrown big cities to embark on the adventure of animating a new town cannot be persuded to think of themselves as city-founders, but persist in thinking of themselves as going into the country, there can, unless population growth-rate can be held down to zero, be only one outcome: a Britain very largely covered with the kind of dismal suburban sprawl which has disfigured the north-eastern States of the United States, and so much of London's surrounding country. In the new towns which we have built in the last few decades, very real efforts have been made to diversify architecture, to avoid the more depressing kind of regularity and rectilinearity of street lay-out. But the creation of neighbourhoods with dwellings all in one 'income bracket' category is encouraging an undesirable class-segregation, and, in the long run, the kind of class fossilization which can lead to something like a caste-system. And, in our context, we are still marring more than we are making Britain's face.

At Harlow new town the planner, Sir Frederick Gibberd, set out deliberately, in his own words, '. . . to preserve and develop the natural features which give the area its particular character; the valleys, brooks, woods, clumps of trees, are all, therefore, retained as "pegs" on which the design is hung'. Admirable though this be, it has, surely, too little to do with the concept 'town' and too much to do with the concept 'suburb'. The rural is being turned into the sub-rural and the sub-rural is equivalent to the suburban. It is true that keeping bits of the country inside the boundaries of the 'town' forced the planner to work to a greater density in the residential neighbourhoods and industrial zones:

[2] F. J. Osborn and A. Whittick, *The New Towns*. London, 1969.

Above: *Harlow new town, Essex, shopping precinct.*

Below: *An aerial view of the new housing at Harlow.*

but the separation between them means that once again the garden suburb and garden city concepts have become confused. Most of the houses are in terraces at fifteen to the acre, each house having a small garden; there are a few semi-detached and even detached houses. Flats are for the most part in three- or four-storey blocks, but there are nine-, ten-, eleven- and twelve-storey blocks and three which go up to fifteen storeys.

Larger than these new towns is another, Basildon, in Essex, which is to have a population of 140,000. The site of about 8,000 acres takes in two older small towns and some villages. The master plan allows for twenty-four neighbourhoods. Despite some efforts to vary house design, the overall effect is flat, bleak and monotonous. Again, the usual consequences of having to plan towns for automan and gardeners has led to that suburban look: because it means too open, too sprawling a plan.

Other new towns added to Britain's face since the end of the war are Bracknell, five miles from White Waltham on the London to Reading line, Newton Aycliffe in south Durham – still building, as are Peterlee in east Durham, Washington between Newcastle and Gateshead and Felling in Sunderland. A good start has been made on Skelmersdale, a new town for 80,000 people from the Liverpool slums. Corby, built round the village of that name in Northamptonshire, is more advanced. Others in various stages of growth are Telford, Redditch, Cymbran in Gwent – the latter more or less complete.

As well as the building of new towns there has been extension of old ones small enough to stand it without losing their unity – Hemel Hempstead, Hatfield and Runcorn are cases in point; and expansion of such quite large towns as Peterborough, Northampton, Warrington and Ipswich.

In all, this amounts to a very large addition of man-made features to Britain's face during the last three decades. But it is as nothing compared with what will have to be done: for, socially, it is totally inadequate. At the time of writing, it is officially admitted that about four and a half million houses in Britain are substandard, and it is well known that a large proportion of these are unfit for human habitation. We must try to get some idea of what the solution of the problem is going to mean for Britain's looks.[3]

[3] Of the West European industrial countries Britain is the most backward in housing, spending less of the gross national product on housing than any other comparable country.

New housing in Basildon.

As far as I can calculate, we have provided for two million people by the building of new towns and expansion of old ones in the post-Second World War period. And it looks very much as if, in the coming five or six decades, we shall have to build new towns or expand old ones to accommodate about ten times that number. And it is not simply a question of building houses or flats: the new people will need factories and offices to work in, more road-room to drive on, more halls and other public buildings to lead their communal life in, more recreation space and buildings, more power-stations to provide them with energy, heat and light, more schools, hospitals and universities. So that the question is not whether we should or should not set about remaking the face of Britain; we are obliged to do so; the only question is how to make it, not mar it.

The skills, taste and talents of our architects and planners would make it possible to turn all Britain into a man-made paradise of true country and true cities, the right setting for the good life. Naturally, there are obstacles, things like high interest rates, selfish property-rights in land with an entirely artificial 'value'; and the illusion that Britain has a particular, immutable and somehow 'right' face which should not be and even cannot be changed. But these could be overcome, given the will and the vision.

We have to face the fact that, going by the population/acreage ratio of the new towns we have built hitherto, and allowing for a foreseeable population increase, and supposing that we still adhere to the garden-suburb style of town building, then *several tens of millions of acres* of what remains of rural Britain are going to be covered with such garden-suburb-like towns.

What alternative is there? If we look at the work of designers and builders of new universities rather than new towns, a different picture emerges: the ratio of space occupied by building to space occupied by parkland round the building is very much lower; and even where this is not literally true, the fact that buildings are in compact blocks, and the land all in one expanse, not broken up into tiny plots, gives a result which, aesthetically, is very much superior. But the people-per-acre ratio is lower. So that, taking such university complexes as a model, and supposing the next generation of new towns to have the compactness of real cities instead of the sprawl of garden-suburbs, much more land would have to be taken and landscaped as park; but much less of it would be covered with a wide scatter of buildings.

Of course, university-style living quarters would not be acceptable

Contrasts. Orvieto, a beautiful Italian hill town – clustered on the side of a steep hill, it commands views in all directions of the wonderful rolling countryside. Opposite above: Sulgrave Village, Washington new town, England.

and I do not suggest that: a people-to-room ratio of 1 : 1 is the lowest acceptable. But that can be accomplished after the style of the new universities – after all, a large university has the population of a small town – rather than after the style of the present generation of new towns. And if something of the kind were to be applied to redevelopment of decayed urban areas, as well as to development, we could have a Britain of beautiful residential-industrial-academic cities, as diverse as our architects could make them using various styles and a wide range of different local materials as well as the universal materials, each one a work of art, and each standing in its own park-cum-farmland.

What would be the advantage of such compact cities, as compact, for example, as the lovely old Tuscan and Umbrian hill-towns? It would be quite easy to exclude the motor-car from inside the city proper, for all movement could be on foot, or by moving-ways of the kind used in certain great airports; and by electric public transport. The citizens would not, therefore, be deprived of their motor-cars, which would be parked outside the city. Compactness without overcrowding favours the growth of civic spirit, and therefore of a true urban community. Compact cities in parks would be in close touch with 'country'; not, to be sure, with wild nature but we have already made it clear that that is no longer really possible in any case; but with a gardened community of plants, animals and birds among lakes, streams and woods. Does it sound impossible? Take Capability Brown's methods; apply to them our

The changing face of English domestic architecture.

modern means – that is, powerful mechanical tools – and the thing could be done easily enough.

As for agriculture, the National Trust have demonstrated on numerous properties, farming need not be excluded from estates open for recreation, nor the public seeking recreation from farmland. And as Capability Brown and Humphry Repton demonstrated nearly two centuries ago, in scores of cases, farms can be incorporated, with aesthetic advantage rather than loss, into landscaped parks. It is true that the farms in the sort of city parks envisaged could not be of the vast, open-prairie kind worked with few hands and huge machines. But nor, on the other hand, need they be archaic: they would certainly be mechanized, using smaller machines; they could use properly 'composted' city wastes for fertilizer (techniques have been pioneered in Scandinavia); and as to manning, there is no reason why urban industrial, office and academic workers should not lend a hand on the farm in certain seasons.

Another point about farming in these conditions: the open-prairie type of farm is more 'efficient' than the smaller, intensively cultivated, well-manned farm only in cost accountants' terms, that is to say in terms of money return per man-hour acre. If the calculations and comparisons be made in terms of return in food value per man-hour acre, the smaller, better-manned farm is more efficient, although not, of course, as efficient as a properly cultivated kitchen-garden. A Wye College (London University) study[4] showed that where the tenants or house-owners on a housing-estate grow vegetables with ordinary care and average success in their gardens, the output of food-per-acre is at least as great as it was before the land was built on, though, of course, the kind of food produced changes.

At the time of writing, we still, despite the fact that about one thousand million people live on the starvation line, tolerate money-return criteria in judging agriculture, the food production industry. But with an explosively rising world population, louder and louder demands from the undernourished for the living standards of the overnourished, and an almost world-wide retreat from farming, it is doubtful if that criterion will long remain tolerable.

What has all this to do with Britain's face? In the future, everything. For the time being I think it socially impossible that we should start to build compact cities in the sort of parks I have sketched; but it may become socially as well as physically impossible to do anything else, to go on covering more and more of the land's face with garden-suburbs. For the time being, that is what we shall go on doing; and the best immediate hope for aesthetically and socially more impressive building is perhaps in the redevelopment rather than the development areas.

Either way we must be sure of one thing: we began, thirty centuries – only about 120 generations – ago to make over nature's Britain to suit our purposes. We shall have to complete the job and make all the face of Britain a work of man: and that means, at best, a great work of art; at worst, a random assemblage of incongruous artefacts.

I have assumed in all this that we shall be able to afford the transformations we need to make. At the start of 1976 the prospect is gloomy. But the crisis is one created by mismanagement, not by any real want of resources. Once we set ourselves to the task of making more intelligent use of our resources we should have the means to do what has to be done.

[4] *The Garden Controversy*. Best & Ward, London, 1956.

Selected Reading List

ASHTON, T. S. *The Industrial Revolution 1760–1830*. Oxford 1948

BEAN, W. J. *Trees and Shrubs Hardy in the British Isles*. London 1934/1973

BERESFORD, M. W. *New Towns in the Middle Ages*. London 1967

CHADWICK, N. K. *Celtic Britain*. London 1963

COLLINGWOOD, R. G. and MYERS, J. N. L. *Roman Britain and the English Settlements*. London 1937

DEFOE, DANIEL. *A Tour through England and Wales*. London (Everyman) 1928

GOTHEIN, M-L. *A History of Garden Art*. London 1966

HADFIELD, M. *Gardening in Britain*. London 1960

HAWKES, J. *A Land*. London 1951

HAWKES, J. and C. *Prehistoric Britain*. London 1944

HOSKINS, W. G. *The Making of the English Landscape*. London 1955

HYAMS, E. *Soil and Civilization*. London 1952

HYAMS, E. *Capability Brown and Humphry Repton*. London 1971

HYAMS, E. *The English Garden*. London 1964

HYAMS, E. and SMITH, E. *The English Cottage Garden*. London 1970

KENCHINGTON, F. E. *The Commoners New Forest*. London 1949

LETCHBRIDGE, T. C. *Boats and Boatmen*. London 1952

MARTIN, E. W. (ed.) *Country Life in England*. London 1966

MORRIS, C. *The Journeys of Celia Fiennes*. London 1947

NEF, J. U. *Essays in Economic History*. Ed. Carus-Wilson, E.M. London 1961

NEF, J. U. *The Rise of the British Coal Industry*. London 1966

NOCK, O. S. *The Railways of Britain Past and Present*. London 1948

ORISH, G. *The Living House*. London 1959

PARKINSON, J. *Paradisus in sole paradisi terrestris*. London 1669

RYAN, P. *The National Trust*. London 1969

SALAMAN, R. *The History and Social Influence of the Potato*. London 1949

SLICKER VAN BATH, B. H. *The Agrarian History of Western Europe 500–1850*. London 1963

TACITUS *Agricola*

VARAGNAC, A. *L'Homme avant l'écriture*. Paris 1968

WILSON, D. M. *The Anglo-Saxons*. London 1965

Acknowledgements

The Author and publishers wish to thank the following for permission to reproduce illustrative material in this volume:

Black and white:

Aerofilms for pages 27, 31, 32, 36 *below*, 44, 51, 65 *above*, 55, 97 *both*, 211, 212, 240, 242 *below*; Aldus Books for page 24; The Ashmolean Museum, Oxford, for pages 34 and 63 *above* (Photos by the late Major G. W. E. Allen), 40 *above*, 57, 61 *above*; Barnaby's Picture Library for pages 209 *above* (Photo by Gerald Wilson), 236, 238 *above* (Photo by Ken Lambert); Basildon Development Corporation for page 242; British Aircraft Corporation for page 216 *below*; The Trustees of The British Museum for pages 28 *above*, 39 (Photo Otto Fein), 47 *below*, 42, 49, 60 *above*, 60 *below*, 107 *above*; British Rail for pages 194, 196 *above*; The British Travel Association for page 76; Central Electricity Generating Board for page 214; Country Life for pages 117, 118, 129, 131, 133, 134; Crawley New Town for page 240 *above*; Department of the Environment (Crown Copyright) for pages 49, *right above*, 51 *above* and *centre*, 53, *above* and *centre*, 53, *below*; Mary Evans Picture Library for pages 147 *above*, 148, 151, 165 *above*, 153, 167; Foto-Enit-Roma for pages 244–245 *above*; Gloucester City Museum for page 44 *above*; Guildhall Museum for page 178 *below*; Haringey Public Library for page 162; Institute of Geological Science (Crown Copyright) for pages 14 *above* and 15 *above*; J. Allan Cash for pages 12, 79, 89, 101 *below*, 212 *below*, 80, 139, 196, 216, 225, 236 *above*; A. F. Kersting for pages 119 *both*, 125, 199 *above*, 139, *below*; Longman Group Ltd for pages 60, 128, 131, 137; Eric Lyons and Partners Architects for pages 230, 233 (Photo by Colin Westwood); The Mansell Collection for pages 53 *centre*, 102 *both*, 101, 142, 144, 147 *below*, 165, 169 *both*, 171; National Monuments Record for pages 85 *above*, 88 *above*, 89 *above* (Photo by F. C. Morgan), 84, 95 *below* (Photos by B. T. Batsford); The National Museum of Wales for page 40 *above*; The National Portrait Gallery for pages 129 *above*, 131 *below*; P and A Photos for pages 14 *both*, 194, 196 *below*, 199, 205, 218, 219, 220 *all three*, 222, 227, 230, 234; Picturepoint Ltd for page 189 *below*; Port of London Authority for page 180 *below*; The Press Association for page 175; Radio Times Hulton Picture Library for pages 17 *below*, 29, 66 (Photo by Herbert Felton), 67, 68, 69 (Photo by Val Doone), 70, 72 *both*, 83, 88, 91, 93, 96 *both*, 107, 109, 173 *above*; The Royal Institute of British Architects for pages 189, 190; The Science Museum, London, for page 180 *above*; *The Times* for page 36 *above*; Thompson Newspapers Ltd for page 157; Victoria and Albert Museum and The Phaidon Press for page 80; Washington Development Corporation for page 245 *above*.

Illustrations by Anthony Colbert are based in part on material from the following sources: Her Majesty's Stationery Office, The Illustrated London News (for page 66), Mary Evans Picture Library, Picturepoint Ltd., Barnaby's Picture Library, Longman Group Ltd., Time-Life Books, The Mansell Collection, and *Art and The Industrial Revolution* by Francis D. Kimender, 1947.

Index